2020
Every Column Ben Shapiro Wrote During an Insane Year

2020

Every Column Ben Shapiro Wrote During an Insane Year

Ben Shapiro

Creators Publishing
Hermosa Beach, CA

CREATORS PUBLISHING
737 3rd St
Hermosa Beach, CA 90254
310-337-7003

ISBN (print): 978-1-949673-55-5
ISBN (ebook): 978-1-949673-54-8

First Edition
Printed in the United States of America
1 3 5 7 9 10 8 6 4 2

A Note From the Publisher

Since 1987, Creators has syndicated many of your favorite columns to newspapers. In this digital age, we are bringing collections of those columns to your fingertips. This will allow you to read and reread your favorite columnists, with your own personal digital archive of their work.

—Creators Publishing

Contents

When Anti-Semitism Doesn't Matter

January 1, 2020

In October 2018, during Sabbath morning services, a white supremacist attacked the Tree of Life synagogue in Pittsburgh, murdering 11 people and wounding another six. In April 2019, in the middle of Passover, a white supremacist attacked the Chabad of Poway synagogue, murdering one person and seriously wounding another three. Both incidents started absolutely necessary conversations about the prevalence and nature of the white supremacist threat to Jews across the country.

Four people were murdered at a kosher supermarket in Jersey City by self-described Black Hebrew Israelites just weeks ago; five people were stabbed at a Hanukkah celebration in Monsey, New York; this week alone, New York police are investigating at least nine anti-Semitic attacks. The upsurge of violence against Jews in New York in particular has finally prompted commentary from Democratic politicians ranging from New York Mayor Bill De Blasio, who just weeks ago expressed shock at anti-Semitism reaching "the doorstep of New York City"; to New York Gov. Andrew Cuomo, who expressed puzzlement at the attacks, noting broadly: "This is an intolerant time in our country. We see anger; we see hatred exploding."

This isn't new. Back in 2018, The New York Times admitted there was a massive spike in anti-Semitic attacks in the city—and even acknowledged that the newspaper of record had failed to cover that surging anti-Semitism because "it refuses to conform to an easy narrative with a single ideological enemy." But that has always been true of anti-Semitism. It's possible, as The Times should recognize, to walk and chew gum at the same time in covering anti-Semitism.

But it's not mere lack of focus and time preventing the media from taking anti-Semitism in New York seriously. It's the identity of the attackers. Armin Rosen wrote for Tablet Magazine back in July 2019 about the Jew hatred in New York and correctly noted "that the victims are most often outwardly identifiable, i.e., religious rather than secularized Jews, and the perpetrators who have been recorded on CCTV cameras are overwhelmingly black and Hispanic." This throws the media—and many left-leaning Jewish organizations—into spasms of confusion, since it cuts directly against the supposed alliance of intersectionality so beloved by the political left. White supremacists attacking left-leaning Jews fits a desired narrative. Black teenagers beating up Hasidic Jews in Williamsburg doesn't.

And so the left ignores the *wrong* type of anti-Semitism.

The same media that will ask whether President Donald Trump's executive orders designed to protect Jews on campus are *ackshually* anti-Semitic will ignore the fact that former President Barack Obama sat in Jeremiah Wright's church for *20 years*—the same Jeremiah Wright who railed against Jews and Israel routinely during those years; who said Jews kept Obama from talking with him after the election; and who avers that "Jesus was a Palestinian." Democratic candidates who suggest that Trump has emboldened anti-Semites will make pilgrimage to Rev. Al Sharpton, who was instrumental in not one but *two* anti-Semitic riots. The same commentators who will police Republican references to George Soros for hints of anti-Semitism completely excuse open anti-Semitism when it comes from Reps. Rashida Tlaib and Ilhan Omar. It's deemed completely vital by our intelligentsia to survey white Americans for signs of white supremacy and, by extension, signs of anti-Semitism. Those same intelligentsia will patently ignore the fact that anti-Semitic attitudes among black Americans *far* outweigh similar attitudes among other racial groups, according to repeated polling by the Anti-Defamation League.

Anti-Semitism grows when the victims become secondary and the perpetrators become primary. If you're only concerned about anti-Semitism from white supremacists but utterly blithe about Jews being beaten in the streets of one of the nation's largest cities by suspects who clearly are not white supremacists, you're part of the problem.

And that goes for those who govern New York, from De Blasio to Cuomo.

Trump's Iran Policy Isn't the Problem; Barack Obama's Was

January 8, 2020

This week, President Donald Trump launched a global round of teeth gnashing when he ordered the killing of the greatest terrorist leader in the modern Middle East, Iranian Maj. Gen. Qasem Soleimani. Soleimani was unquestionably responsible for the deaths of hundreds of Americans in Iraq and thousands of others throughout the Middle East—mostly Muslim. His global terror network ran from South America to Europe to Africa to Lebanon, Syria, Yemen and Iraq. Soleimani was an unparalleled organizer and a pitiless murderer. His death was richly earned.

But for many in the media and on the domestic and international left, Trump's action was precipitously "provocative." House Speaker Nancy Pelosi called Soleimani's killing—which came directly after a Soleimani-approved terror assault on America's embassy in Baghdad and amidst reported further plans for escalated terror against American targets—"disproportionate." Sen. Elizabeth Warren, D-Mass., suggested that Trump, not the Iranians, had "escalated" the situation. Former Vice President Joe Biden said that Trump had "just tossed a stick of dynamite into a tinderbox."

This reaction has been magnified by the media, many of whom have been speculating about the possibility of all-out war between the United States and Iran. Think pieces have been written about whether the United States will reactivate the draft (spoiler alert: No, we won't). Musings have filled the newspapers about the supposed conflagration prompted not by Iranian evil but by Trumpian reactivity.

All of this smacks less of legitimate concern about what comes next than it does of sheer panic that Trump has overturned a decade of American and European appeasement of the Iranian regime. Ben Rhodes, former President Obama's deputy national security adviser, architect of the Iran deal and an overt liar who told the American public that Iran was on its way to moderation if only the United States would loosen economic restrictions on the terror state, has placed blame for volatility squarely before Trump. Susan Rice, Obama's national security adviser during the Iran deal and another overt liar who told the American public that Islamic terror against our Benghazi embassy was rooted in anger over a YouTube video, soberly informed Americans that "Americans would be wise to brace for war." Biden suggested that in throwing out the Iran deal, Trump had paved the way for war—and, oh, by the way, the Iran deal was "airtight."

This is a deliberate misreading of history designed to absolve the Obama administration of its Iran policy debacle. The administration pursued a policy of strengthening Iran economically—and did so while openly acknowledging that Iran would use that newly gained economic strength to pursue terrorism and ballistic missile testing. In speaking of the sanctions relief given to Iran, then-Secretary of State John Kerry explained in January 2016, "I think that some of it will end up in the hands of the IRGC or other entities, some of which are labeled terrorists."

That's precisely what happened. In March 2016, then-U.S. Central Command nominee Army Gen. Joseph Votel said that Iran had become "more aggressive" since the advent of the nuclear deal. Indeed, Iran has built up Hezbollah in Lebanon, propped up Bashar Assad in Syria, increased its presence in Iraq and bolstered its war in Yemen. In the past few months, Iran and its proxies have attacked shipping in the Strait of Hormuz, Saudi oil facilities, an American drone and an American embassy, among other targets. All of this occurred while the Trump administration did little or nothing in response.

Then Trump ordered the killing of Soleimani. Suddenly, we have been informed by dishonest Democrats and their media allies, Iran has gone rogue.

Nonsense. Iran has been rogue for decades. The Iran deal was simply an attempt to whistle past the graveyard with the terror regime—to pay it off long enough so that President Barack Obama could declare the problem handled. This was, after all, the Obama strategy in Crimea and Syria: Declare a red line; run away from it; pretend that pusillanimous inaction is bravery and deterrence provocation.

Trump thought differently. Now Iran has come face to face with the prospect that actions have consequences—and those consequences don't involve pallets of cash being shipped over to fund terror organizations that span the globe.

The Perpetual Intersectional Revolution Eats Its Own

January 15, 2020

In 2008, Democrats nominated for president a first-term U.S. senator with no serious legislative experience, Barack Obama. They nominated him over the long-championed, long-celebrated presumptive heir apparent to the Democratic leadership, Hillary Clinton. Obama was, of course, the first black Democratic nominee, and he would be the first black president.

Yet in 2020, 12 years later, we have been informed by the media that Democrats are ensconced in racism anew. Why? First, because Democrats refused to activate in support of awkwardly robotic Sen. Kamala Harris, D-Calif., who is black; second, because Democrats refused to activate in support of wild-eyed former Secretary of Housing and Urban Development Julian Castro, who is Latino; and now because Democrats refused to activate in support of scenery-chewing Sen. Cory Booker, D-N.J., who is black. Democrats have been accused by the media of having ignored their initially diverse field in favor of old, white candidates (amusingly, the media only noticed that Sen. Elizabeth Warren was, indeed, an old white person when actual people of color were booted from the race). It appears that the memory of President Obama—not yet four years old—is not enough to insulate Democrats from charges of discrimination.

Then there's Hollywood.

In 2014, African actress Lupita Nyong'o won an Oscar for her supporting role in "12 Years a Slave." In 2018, director Greta Gerwig was nominated for a best director Oscar for "Lady Bird." Yet this week, we found out that the Academy of Motion Picture Arts and

Sciences had neglected—horror of horrors!—to nominate both Nyong'o, for her role in the extraordinarily overrated horror flick "Us," and Gerwig, for her direction of "Little Women." These oversights, we were solemnly informed, evidenced the Academy's deep-seated bias in favor of white men. Never mind that Cynthia Erivo was nominated for best actress for her role as Harriet Tubman in "Harriet." Discrimination was alive and well in Hollywood.

It must be difficult to live in an environment in which every day is a perpetual test of one's submission to the Woke Police. It must be difficult to know that no past act stands in favor of the accused—that each day must be lived fresh—and that all past omissions stand against the accused. But the intersectional revolution requires continual struggle, and continual sacrifice.

In Arthur Koestler's "Darkness at Noon," communist lackey Rubashov is jailed and charged—of what crime, it does not matter. The Soviet Union is purging members of the older generation, and Rubashov is told that he must confess in order to uphold the sanctity of his own cause. Eventually, Rubashov does exactly that. "There is nothing for which one could die, if one died without having repented and unreconciled with the Party and the Movement," Rubashov says in his confession. "Therefore, on the threshold of my last hour, I bend my knees to the country, to the masses and to the whole people." The choice between dying honestly, in repudiation of his own cause, was simply too much.

In the end, all revolutionaries will have to determine whether they, too, will bow before the cause—even if they go unjustly to the guillotine. Because there is one basic rule of radical revolutions: Those who are first to launch them are often just *slightly* delayed in feeling their wrath.

The Alexandria Ocasio-Cortez
School of Economics

January 22, 2020

On Monday, Rep. Alexandria Ocasio-Cortez, D-N.Y., sat for a discussion with author Ta-Nehisi Coates. She dropped a number of shocking statements—statements that elicited nothing but murmurs of agreement from Coates. AOC claimed: "No one ever makes a billion dollars. You take a billion dollars." How, pray tell, are American billionaires responsible for such massive theft? According to AOC, the very mechanisms of capitalism mandate such theft. In her view, successful businesspeople simply exploit their workers while maximizing their profits. Hypothetically speaking about billionaires making widgets, she said: "You didn't make those widgets! You sat on a couch while thousands of people were paid modern-day slave wages and, in some cases, real modern-day slavery ... You made that money off the backs of undocumented people."

This, of course, is nonsense. Voluntary exchange of labor for wages is, as stated, *voluntary*, and the fact that there are many people willing and able to labor in the manufacture of widgets is presumably responsible for lower wages. Companies that refuse to pay their workers market wages will soon watch those workers migrate to other businesses or other industries. It is a patent violation of free market principles to utilize force in order to compel someone to work for you; blaming the free market for coercion is like blaming free speech for censorship. Exploitation in labor markets is typically accompanied by government subsidies, regulation and interventionism.

So, how does AOC magically turn economic freedom into economic tyranny? By suggesting that *true* freedom lies in collective control of the means of production: "If you're a billionaire, that means that you control a massive system. ... It means that you have a massive labor force under your control, and to be ethical if you're a billionaire today, the thing that you need to do is give up control and power." But to whom would such power and control be given? AOC suggests that major companies be turned into worker cooperatives—companies whose workers own and control the business.

But, of course, that doesn't solve her problem: If workers own and control the business, they are properly classified as capitalists. They will have to make decisions to make the business competitive, which means keeping wages competitive, for example. This is precisely what has happened with one of the world's biggest worker collectives, the Spanish Mondragon Cooperative Corporation, whose worker-owners have "learned to think like the shareholders of any other global business," according to The Guardian. In fact, most companies begin with a few workers who pool their capital and labor: Facebook, for example, handed out stock options to employees, resulting in a $23 billion valuation for their initial employees when the company went public. Does that make those workers evil capitalists?

In the end, what AOC *truly* wants is government control. Worker collectives won't do the trick. Only top-down government redefinition of the value of labor will. When AOC claims that capitalists merely leech off the *true* value of labor, she suggests that labor can be measured without reference to the market. How would AOC measure the value of such labor? Presumably through appeals to "fairness." There is only one problem with this method: It simply doesn't work. Consumers determine the value of products; producers do not. The diffuse informational system of the free market, which rewards the power of entrepreneurship, rather than punishing it, creates prosperity; top-down control creates poverty. In fact, the greatest guarantee of the sort of poverty AOC decries is the destruction of the same system she decries.

But according to AOC, we have nothing to fear from government, and "the government is us." The fact that Coates, one of the most prominent writers on the evils of Jim Crow, nodded along should demonstrate that those on the left do not understand the consequences of their own philosophy. The government is not "us," because *we* are not a collective. We are individuals with rights. But in AOC's world, we have no rights—we have only our role as members of a collective controlled by those who agree with her. And that *is* exploitation and tyranny.

When 'Never Again' Means Nothing

January 29, 2020

This week, the world marked the 75th anniversary of the liberation of Auschwitz by Allied forces during World War II. Politicians of all stripes dutifully tweeted, "#NeverAgain." Meanwhile, many of those same politicians continued to forward the worst sort of anti-Semitism, blithely ignoring the fact that anti-Semitism isn't a relic of the past but a thriving part of the present.

Take, for example, Rep. Ilhan Omar, D-Minn. Omar has, in the past two years alone, sponsored an anti-Semitic resolution that likened boycotts of Israel to boycotts of Nazi Germany; rejected a Democratic-sponsored resolution backing a two-state solution in order to chide the Trump administration and Israel, because the solution wasn't radical enough; and repeatedly suggested that Jewish money manipulates American foreign policy on Israel. Her anti-Semitism was so palpable that the Democrats were forced to debate and then water down a resolution condemning anti-Semitism. Still, Omar tweeted, "Today and every day, we must redouble our efforts to confront anti-Semitism and all forms of religious discrimination and say #NeverAgain."

Or how about Rep. Rashida Tlaib, D-Mich.? She tweeted a story about a Holocaust survivor visiting Auschwitz and added, "May we honor them by sharing stories like these, #NeverAgain allowing hate to flourish, and committing to speaking out against anti-Semitism and all other forms of hate." Just two days before that tweet, Tlaib put out a now-deleted retweet of anti-Semitic blood libel that accused "a Herd of violent #Israeli settlers" of kidnapping a 7-year-old boy and drowning him in a well. In reality, the boy was 8 years old and apparently had drowned after slipping into a pool of rainwater in the

Beit Hanina neighborhood. Tlaib, of course, is no stranger to Jew hatred: In the past two years, she has accused congressional lawmakers opposed to the boycott, divestment and sanctions movement of dual loyalty and hobnobbed with open terror supporters, and she is the bedrock congressional supporter of BDS itself. Both Tlaib and Omar have provided moral support for Hamas, the terror group in charge of the Gaza Strip.

Then there's Jeremy Corbyn, the British Labour Party leader who so disgraced his own party with his coddling of anti-Semites that he was rejected by many members of his upper echelon. Corbyn glibly tweeted, "This is a time for us all to reflect on the horrors of the past, the evils of Nazism, genocide and antisemitism, and indeed all forms of racism, which we must always be determined to root out, wherever they appear."

The truth is that #NeverAgain has become a virtue signal for many on the modern left, who are more than willing to greenlight the genocidal anti-Semitism of Hamas, Hezbollah, the Palestinian Authority and the Iranian regime, among others. Islamic anti-Semitism, in their view, is not true anti-Semitism; it's just religious conflict, or territorial disagreement, or anti-Zionism. When such ideological disagreements result in open calls for the murder of Jews ... well, that's going a bit too far, but it's understandable. After all, modern Jews—particularly Zionists, who insist on a Jewish state to ensure the survival of their people—are rather bothersome in real life, unlike those dead Jews from World War II, who aren't any more real than their old black-and-white photos, and whose survival is no longer at issue.

It's easy for radical leftists and their Islamic allies to spout #NeverAgain while proclaiming that today's Jews aren't like yesterday's Jews. All of which is why Israel's continued existence provides both a thorn in the side of modern anti-Semites and why Israel's continued existence is so necessary. Vague expressions of upset over an event that took place 75 years ago are no substitute for the hard-nosed defense of Jewish survival that Israel represents. And Jews should remember that when they decide to blind themselves to the real and present anti-Semitism of the Omars, Tlaibs and Corbyns.

Why the Democrats Won't Stop Bernie

February 4, 2020

There is no doubt that Sen. Bernie Sanders, I-Vt., is now the leading Democratic presidential candidate. That's not because his ideas are overwhelmingly popular—a majority of Americans approve of capitalism, while less than 1 in 5 like socialism; few Americans are on board with total nationalization of health care, even if many like the idea of universal health care; most Americans do not approve of Sanders' anti-American ideology with regard to foreign policy.

But nobody in the Democratic Party can stop Bernie.

There's a reason for this: The Democratic Party has fed off the energy of Sanders' ideology hoping that, eventually, the voters would come to their senses. Leading candidates have echoed Sanders' talking points. Sen. Elizabeth Warren adopted and then abandoned Medicare for All, and former Vice President Joe Biden mirrored Sanders' Howard Zinn historical perspective. Those who have attempted to siphon off Sanders' base and approximate his authenticity have failed dramatically.

Instead, Sanders continues to resonate with the base. After all, if you're going to go with an anti-Constitution, anti-free market, intersectionality-based perspective, why water it down with insincerity? Sanders brags about the fact that his ideology has never changed. He's right. Back in 1976, he suggested that he favored "the public ownership of utilities, banks and major industries." He sounded off for decades on the glories of communist Cuba and the Soviet Union; he basked in the joys of bread lines, saying: "In other countries, people don't line up for food. The rich get the food, and the poor starve to death." Sanders trots out campaign surrogates who openly claim that the United States is rooted in genocide and racism, and that the American system must be fundamentally remade.

This is radical stuff. But radicals have passion. And politicians of the Democratic Party are unwilling to quell that passion—not when they believe they can capture it and turn it against President Donald Trump. This is the mirror image of the Republican problem with Trump in 2016: Trump ran on a platform of bashing the Iraq War and America's intelligence agencies, blasting free trade, pledging to avoid entitlement program reforms and slamming the door on immigration. Instead of fighting those elements, Republicans decided to tinge their own campaigns with those attitudes and then assume Trump would collapse under the weight of his own personality flaws. That never happened.

Democrats seem to be waiting for another collapse that simply isn't coming. Sanders isn't going anywhere. His floor is high, and his ceiling remains low—just like Trump. Electability problems aren't going to dissuade his supporters, who believe—correctly—that inauthenticity provides its own electoral issues.

There was another path. Some Democrat could have completely and utterly rejected Sanders' perspective on the world. Some Democrat could have rejected Sanders' view that America has been a nefarious force in the world; some Democrat could have argued that America isn't perfect but that it has always been great; some Democrat could have talked about the wonders of the free market while arguing for greater strictures on it. After all, the majority of Democrats count themselves as patriots who don't despise the free market.

But no Democrat was willing to stand up to the Sanders base. They were too greedy for its energy, and too optimistic that the energy was transferable. It wasn't. And so the Democratic Party has been captured by an ideology foreign to it—the ideology of Noam Chomsky infused directly into the bloodstream of a party that once touted former President John F. Kennedy. Partisanship is a hell of a drug.

The Glorious Alternative Reality of Leftism

February 12, 2020

In 1966, there were 654 murders in New York City. The next year, that number increased by about a hundred. Then two hundred. By the mid-1970s, nearly 1,700 people were being murdered every year in New York City. That insane level of violence maintained until the early 1990s. Then, in 1994, the level of murder in New York City began to decline. It declined from approximately 2,000 people killed in 1993 to 289 in 2018—a level not seen since the end of World War II. Needless to say, on a per capita basis, the murder rate had never been that low.

What, exactly, happened in the early 1990s? New York City residents were simply tired of living in a crime haven. They elected Rudy Giuliani mayor, and Giuliani pledged to enforce the so-called broken windows theory to clean up so-called quality-of-life crimes, stating: "It's the street tax paid to drunks and panhandlers. It's the squeegee men shaking down the motorist waiting at a light. It's the trash storms, the swirling mass of garbage left by peddlers and panhandlers, and open-air drug bazaars on unclean streets." In April 1994, Giuliani's New York Police Department implemented Compstat, a data-driven program designed to deploy police to the highest-crime areas, preemptively targeting criminality, rather than reacting to it. Chris Smith of New York Magazine gushed, "No New York invention, arguably, has saved more lives in the past 24 years." The NYPD also began to employ the "stop, question and frisk" policy, designed to allow police officers to spot people suspected of criminally carrying weapons and frisk them for those weapons after questioning.

New York turned from a mess into a haven. But now Michael Bloomberg—Giuliani's mayoral successor beginning in 2002—is paying the price for a successful anti-crime record that followed in Giuliani's footsteps. Bloomberg has defended NYPD policies as non-racially biased; in 2015, he told The Aspen Institute that supposedly disproportionate "targeting" of minorities was not disproportionate but based on criminal conduct and description thereof. In crude and insensitive but statistically accurate terminology, Bloomberg pointed out that "Ninety-five percent of your murders and murderers and murder victims fit one M.O. ... They are male minorities 15 to 25." This may have been a slight exaggeration, but only a slight one. In 2008, for example, 88.6% of murder and non-negligent manslaughter victims in New York were black or Hispanic, and 92.8% of murder and non-negligent manslaughter suspects were black or Hispanic, according to New York government statistics. And black and Hispanic suspects were actually *under-arrested*: By these same statistics, just 83.9% of arrestees for murder and non-negligent manslaughter were black or Hispanic.

Nonetheless, Bloomberg was widely blasted as a racist for his comments. That criticism came from both left and right. Bloomberg quickly apologized for his five-year-old comments, saying: "By the time I left office, I cut it back 95%, but I should've done it faster and sooner. I regret that and I have apologized." But Bloomberg should have stood up on his hind legs and *defended one of his only successful poli*cies.

Unfortunately, we live in a world where the counterfactual can be entertained without reference to reality. Thus, we are informed that broken-windows policing, Compstat, and stop and frisk should never have been employed—and we are blithely told that even without those policies, crime would have precipitously dropped over the course of two decades. There is precisely zero evidence to support this supposition, but that's the beauty of writing alternative histories: No evidence is necessary.

The same is true in the world of economics, where Bernie Sanders can spend his days living off the largesse of capitalism—the man has a lake house—while decrying the evils of capitalism. It's easy to proclaim adherence to socialistic redistribution while living high on the hog of the free market. It's shockingly easy to get away with maintaining that American prosperity would not have been undercut by policies precisely the opposite of the policies that have driven American prosperity for centuries.

The joy of alternative realities is that they can't be disproved. We can never disprove the supposition that without anti-crime measures, crime would have dropped anyway; we can never disprove the supposition that without the free market, America would have prospered even more greatly than it has. The acid test of reality never applies to a world in which bad ideas were rejected for more effective ones. Which is why Bernie Sanders, who has produced zero things of consequence for decades but has successfully mooched off the public dime for nearly that entire period, may become president, while Michael Bloomberg, who has produced thousands of jobs and presided over a massive decline in crime in New York City, is in the hot seat.

Michael Bloomberg and the
Politics of Money

February 19, 2020

Former New York Mayor Michael Bloomberg has been rising drastically in the national polling for the 2020 Democratic presidential nomination. Frightened by that rise, Democratic candidates from center-left to communist have risen as one, declaring that Bloomberg has done the process dirty: By dropping hundreds of millions of dollars on advertising, he has thwarted the process, and thus, the will of the people. Sen. Elizabeth Warren, D-Mass., proclaimed: "It's a shame Mike Bloomberg can buy his way into the debate. But at least now primary voters curious about how each candidate will take on Donald Trump can get a live demonstration of how we each take on an egomaniac billionaire." And former Vice President Joe Biden stated, "Sixty billion dollars can buy you a lot of advertising, but it can't erase your record."

All of which raises a serious question: Is Bloomberg doing something deeply wrong—is he "cheating"—by spending oodles of his own money on political advertising?

The answer, of course, is no. Tom Steyer, another Democratic billionaire, has spent over $200 million on political advertising, with little response—he won 0.3% of votes in Iowa and 3.6% of votes in New Hampshire. Bloomberg is resonating because he is vying for the moderate lane in the Democratic primaries just as Biden, the wire-to-wire front-runner until the primaries actually began, flamed out completely. Money, obviously, isn't everything.

But, say the critics, dollars can buy you an entry ticket into the political race. That's undoubtedly true. Dollars plus a political case is better than no dollars plus a political case. But it's also true that dollars become increasingly important in a political system in which candidates can gain outsized attention and vote share by spending money that *doesn't belong to them*. Bloomberg, to his credit, is spending his own money. Sen. Bernie Sanders, I-Vt., and Warren are pledging to spend everyone else's. "Stop trying to buy elections!" rings hollow from a cast of characters who have promised Americans "free" health care, "free" college tuition, "free" child care and "free" housing, among other giveaways.

It also rings hollow from people who have received hundreds of millions of dollars' worth of attention from their like-minded allies in the media. Sanders has earned hundreds of millions of dollars in media attention; so, too, has Warren. Our media act as attention-providing political gatekeepers. For Bloomberg to end-around them is hardly illegitimate.

In truth, the problem for Democrats isn't Bloomberg's spending. The problem is that the Democratic Party now treats wealth itself as an indicator of immorality. This week, Sanders tweeted, "Together, we are going to end the greed of the billionaire class." Never mind that creating tens of billions of dollars in value via voluntary exchange, employing tens of thousands of people, and providing goods and services to millions is far less indicative of greed than living as a taxpayer-funded, parasitical, self-styled revolutionary for six decades. The size of Bloomberg's bank account makes him morally suspect in the world of the modern Democratic Party. There's a reason former South Bend Mayor Pete Buttigieg keeps telling debate crowds that he's the poorest candidate running, as though lack of financial success is a tremendous indicator of governing ability. As Trevor Noah recently joked, being called a wealthy person is, for "progressive white people ... like being called the N-word."

This perspective represents the reversal of the American dream: We should all aspire to government dependency, patting our own backs for our altruism while drawing on the public dime. After all, if wealth is sin, then chiding the wealthy while living off of them is sainthood. That's the Democratic line going into 2020. We'll see soon enough whether Americans are willing to give up the true American dream in favor of yelling at billionaires.

The Worship of Dictators

February 26, 2020

This week, Sen. Bernie Sanders, I-Vt., the socialist Democratic presidential front-runner, made waves when he merely reiterated his lifelong warmth toward the viciously evil Cuban communist regime. Brushing off the human rights violations of Fidel Castro—a man whose revolution ended with the murder or imprisonment of tens of thousands of his countrymen, and decades of impoverishment and repression for millions—Sanders explained: "We're very opposed to the authoritarian nature of Cuba, but you know, it's unfair to simply say everything is bad. ... When Fidel Castro came into office, you know what he did? He had a massive literacy program. Is that a bad thing, even though Fidel Castro did it?"

But, of course, Sanders hasn't merely praised Castro's literacy programs (which, by the way, were propagandistic exploits. Cuba had an 80% literacy rate before Castro's coup). Back in the 1980s, Sanders explained that he was "physically nauseated" by former President John F. Kennedy's "hatred for the Cuban revolution." In 1989, Sanders stated after visiting Cuba: "I did not see a hungry child. I did not see any homeless people." He said that the Cuban people "had an almost religious affection" for Castro.

As it turns out, there is hardly a single communist regime of the past half-century for which Sanders has not expressed some level of moral support. This week, Sanders went out of his way to praise China, explaining: "It's is an authoritarian country. ... But can anyone deny—I mean, the facts are clear—that they have taken more people out of extreme poverty than any country in history?" Naturally, Sanders neglects to mention that China's embrace of free trade and profit margin in the 1990s was responsible for that rise from poverty. That would cut against his socialist worldview.

Then there's the Nicaraguan communist regime of Daniel Ortega, which murdered thousands. Sanders celebrated the Sandinista revolution in the 1980s (he attended a rally at which protesters chanted, "the Yankee will die"), visited Nicaragua and returned to tut-tut Ortega's human rights abuses by citing Abraham Lincoln's suspension of habeas corpus. It's no wonder Ortega has endorsed Sanders for the presidency.

Or how about the Venezuelan regime? Sanders refused to call socialist dictator Nicolas Maduro a dictator as late as last year, and refused to call opposition Juan Guaido the legitimate leader of the country. The Sanders Senate website carried an editorial for years that favorably compared the regime of Hugo Chavez with the poverty record of the United States.

And, of course, there's Sanders' long record of propagandizing on behalf of the Soviet regime. Not only did Sanders visit the Soviet Union for a honeymoon/business trip with his new wife in 1988; he returned and declared that Moscow had "the most effective mass transit system" he had ever seen. He then celebrated that the Soviets were moving "forward into some of the early visions of their revolution, what their revolution was about in 1917."

Sanders isn't a European social democrat, warm toward Denmark and Norway. He's a lifelong communist—a man who declared himself fully on board with the nationalization of nearly every major American industry in the 1970s—and an advocate for anti-Americanism abroad. The fact that it has taken until the verge of his nomination as the 2020 Democratic presidential nominee for members of the media and fellow Democrats to take note of this rather important truth demonstrates that the left's gatekeeping function has been irrevocably broken.

Why Americans Should Celebrate Biden's Comeback

March 4, 2020

On Super Tuesday, the Democratic Party came to its senses—at least, to a point.

Through the first three primaries, Democratic voters seemed sanguine about the possibility of a lifelong communist fellow traveler taking their presidential nomination. Conventional wisdom—including, I admit, my own—suggested that Sen. Bernie Sanders', I-Vt., early primary victories had put former Vice President Joe Biden on the road to ruin. After all, no presidential candidate of the last several election cycles has won after declaring a firewall, from Rudy Giuliani's Florida firewall in 2008 to Hillary Clinton's 2016 blue wall.

But something happened on the way to a Sanders nomination: Democratic voters realized that Bernie Sanders is Bernie Sanders.

It began in South Carolina, where Biden skunked Sanders, outpacing the poll numbers by leaps and bounds. Late-deciding voters simply turned away from Sanders in droves. The same held true on Super Tuesday, when voters across the country ran from Sanders—and from Michael Bloomberg, who acted as a backup choice to Biden and became superfluous the moment Biden showed signs of life in South Carolina. Biden's victories across the South weren't unexpected. His victories in Minnesota, Maine and Massachusetts certainly were.

Biden didn't suddenly reinvigorate his campaign because he became a better campaigner—the day before Super Tuesday, he called Super Tuesday "Super Thursday" and quoted the Declaration of Independence with this immortal formulation: "We hold these truths to be self-evident: All men and women created by the—go—you know—you know the thing!"

Usually, such gaffes are not the sign of a campaign on the upswing.

But for Biden, none of that mattered. That's because once Sanders moved from being the outsider crazy uncle who shouts at clouds to the front-runner, Democratic voters truly had to assess his credentials. Years of media running cover for Sanders made Sanders vulnerable to revelations about his record; the first time Sanders was asked to his face about his lake house was when Michael Bloomberg asked him in a public debate. And Sanders, being a man out of time—that time being 1930s City College of New York—proved unwilling to moderate his extreme views. Instead, he doubled down on his tut-tutting of communist repression, his hatred of Israel and his desire to quash the greatest functioning economy in world history.

And Democrats turned away. Some Democrats were unwilling to stake their 2020 hopes on a Marxist near octogenarian; more were simply unwilling to hand the party over to a Noam Chomsky on foreign policy and a Eugene Debs on domestic policy. Most Democrats still like the United States.

And that's excellent news for the country. A Sanders nomination would have meant, practically speaking, half the country rallying around the agenda of a man who once declared he hoped to nationalize every major industry in the United States, a man who has spent decades praising nearly every communist dictatorship on the planet, a man who seethes with disdain for American history and founding principles. Instead, Democrats will rally around the banner that is anti-President Donald Trump—but Biden isn't an anti-American communist, and his nomination won't mean the deepening of Sanders' vile worldview.

Republicans and Democrats should both celebrate Sanders' precipitous fall. It means that perhaps we still have something in common after all: opposition to a radical philosophy that sees America as a nefarious force in the world and sees constitutional principles as oppressive hierarchical dominance.

What the Coronavirus Should Teach Us

March 11, 2020

As the markets have plummeted over global fears surrounding the fallout from the new coronavirus, political pundits have taken up the call: Find some meaning in the coronavirus outbreak and response. And where there is a demand for speculative opinion, there's never a shortage of supply. Thus we've seen the coronavirus, which originated in Wuhan, China, be blamed on President Donald Trump. We've seen government-managed response, which has varied widely in terms of success by country, touted as a final rebuttal of libertarian precepts. We've seen the coronavirus' economic impact cited as a rationale for breaking global supply chains and pursuing industrial autarky instead.

None of these takeaways are particularly compelling. The Trump administration's response has been about as strong as prior federal attempts to deal with public epidemics, ranging from SARS to swine flu. While Trump himself hasn't exactly projected a sense of calming administrative competence, those around him, ranging from Dr. Anthony Fauci of the National Institute of Allergy and Infectious Diseases to U.S. Surgeon General Dr. Jerome Adams, are fully capable of performing as needed. Libertarianism does not suggest that collective action ought to be out of bounds in the case of public emergencies with serious externalities—few libertarians oppose police departments or proper environmental regulations, for example—and the record of government competence has been, at best, rather mixed. The solution to vulnerable supply chains running through authoritarian countries is, first, for Western countries to consider security threats when formulating trade policy, and second, for companies to harden their supply chains by diversifying those chains *even further.*

So, what are the real lessons to be learned from the coronavirus?

First, we should favor governments that are transparent in their distribution of information. China has been celebrated for its extraordinary crackdown on public life, which has brought transmissions down dramatically. But if it were not for China's propagandistic efforts to quash news about the coronavirus in the first place, the epidemic probably would not have become a pandemic.

Second, we must stop humoring anti-scientific rumormongering about issues like vaccines. The curbing of the coronavirus will be reliant on the development of a vaccine, and Americans should understand that vaccines work, and that misinformation about vaccinations should generally be rejected.

Third, we should remember that crises exacerbate underlying issues; they rarely create them. Economic volatility in the aftermath of the coronavirus has merely exposed the underlying weaknesses of the Chinese and European economies; those systemic problems won't be solved through Band-Aid solutions. The public health issues with homelessness will likely be exposed dramatically in the United States; they won't go away when the coronavirus ends. The coronavirus should underscore the necessity for action in the absence of crisis.

Finally, we should remember that charity and local community support matter. Large-scale government response will never be as efficient or as personal as local response. Care for our neighbors. Care for our families. Implement personal behavior that lowers risk. And then wait for more information. Perhaps that's the best lesson from all of this: Jumping to conclusions based on lack of information is a serious mistake.

Coronavirus Is the 'Chinese Virus'

March 18, 2020

This week, President Donald Trump came under fire for his use of the phrase "Chinese virus" to describe the coronavirus, the source of the new pandemic that has led to a global economic shutdown as well as lockdowns of citizens in every major Western country. That media have somehow found time to hone in on the one issue that matters least—the labeling of a Chinese virus as such—in the middle of an unprecedented planetwide freeze demonstrates the utter unseriousness of those objecting. That the term should be controversial at all is nearly beyond belief. The virus did indeed originate in China. Most of all, that the Chinese government should be shielded in any way from the results of its own pathological and tyrannical misgovernment is perverse beyond measure.

Make no mistake: The Chinese government is chiefly responsible for the explosion of this pandemic. The so-called wet markets of China—the meat markets that often include wild animals ranging from snakes to pangolins—exist for a variety of reasons, ranging from price to superstitious belief in medicinal properties of exotic animals. According to Zhenzhong Si, research associate at the University of Waterloo, "Eating wild animal is considered a symbol of wealth because they are more rare and expensive." Whatever the rationale, the communist Chinese government has been exceedingly tolerant of such markets, even though they have now been responsible for the spread of coronavirus, SARS, bird flu, Asian flu and swine fever. The Chinese government has been similarly tolerant of treatment via traditional Chinese medicine rather than evidence-based medicine, which has increased the risk of such diseases.

The same Chinese government now being praised for its extraordinary crackdown on its own citizens—the same government that is said to be imprisoning up to a million Uighurs for no specific crimes—has been unwilling for decades to stop the selling of exotic animals. Authoritarianism obviously doesn't apply to the most obvious solution to a bevy of possible epidemics.

Meanwhile, the Chinese government acted early to shut down the spread of information about the coronavirus, which paved the way for freedom of travel by carriers of the disease. When ophthalmologist Li Wenliang told fellow doctors about coronavirus in an online chat room in December, he was forced to swear by the Chinese government that he had been making "untrue statements." He ended up dying of the disease. When further information began to emerge about the coronavirus, the communist government simply lied about it, suggesting that case numbers were not rising—a lie bought by the World Health Organization.

Even now the Chinese government continues to spread propaganda suggesting that the coronavirus originated in the United States. Lijian Zhao, deputy director-general of the Information Department of China's Foreign Ministry, tweeted a link to an article he claimed had "Evidence that the Virus Originated in the US." And is it truly believable that China had just 127 diagnosed cases of coronavirus between March 9 and March 16, even as the Chinese government expels American journalists en masse from both China and Hong Kong?

Once this is all over, it's far past time for Americans to have a serious discussion about the extent to which openness to China ought to be curbed. The Trump administration should consider a travel ban on China until China has verifiably shut down its exotic animals markets, at the very least. The current crisis will cost millions of American jobs, millions more of Americans' savings and thousands of American lives. To trust the Chinese government after a global betrayal of this magnitude would not only be foolish; it would be immoral.

America Needs a Formula for Reopening

March 25, 2020

This week, President Donald Trump began openly considering at what point the American government ought to take steps to reopen the American economy. He explained: "Our country wasn't built to be shut down. America will again and soon be open for business," suggesting that the timeline will be weeks instead of months. "If it were up to the doctors," Trump said, "they'd say, 'Let's shut down the entire world.' This could create a much bigger problem than the problem that you started with." Later, Trump optimistically proclaimed that he "would love to have the country opened up and just raring to go by Easter."

Trump's projections drew fire—as do all of his statements. These statements, however, caused inordinate faux heartburn among commentators, who shouted that Trump was weighing dollars against lives and deciding in favor of dollars. The hashtag #NotDyingForWallStreet began trending on Twitter, followed by the hashtag #DieForTheDow. New York Gov. Andrew Cuomo tweeted: "My mother is not expendable. Your mother is not expendable. We will not put a dollar figure on human life. ... No one should be talking about social darwinism for the sake of the stock market." Presumptive 2020 Democratic nominee Joe Biden said, "I don't agree with the notion that somehow it's OK ... to let people die."

That, of course, was not Trump's suggestion. Trump was merely pointing out—quite correctly—that since the federal government has now taken the unprecedented and justifiable action of completely shutting down the American economy, to the tune of millions of lost jobs and the greatest quarterly economic decline in recorded history, we must also have a plan to end this situation.

The economy cannot remain shuttered indefinitely; the federal government cannot engage in endless cash expenditures on the basis of treasuries nobody is buying. Nor is the economy merely Wall Street. The vast majority of those who will lose their jobs are not day traders but workers. Small companies are more likely to go under than large ones. The economy isn't an abstraction. It's the real lives of hundreds of millions of American citizens, and costs to those Americans must be weighed in the balance.

That's not controversial. That's a simple fact. Public policy is the craft of weighing risks and rewards, and policymakers do it every day. It's just that this time, the stakes are the highest they have ever been.

So, when do we reopen, and how?

The biggest problem is that we lack the data to answer the question. How many lives will be lost if we take heavy social measures after how many weeks? Moderate social measures? What will be the concomitant economic gain or loss? How many additional ICU beds and ventilators will we need to make available in order to clear the flattened curve such that we do not experience excess deaths due to lack of equipment, a la Italy? Our goal should be to move from the Chinese model—total lockdown—to the South Korean model—heavy testing, contact investigations and social distancing. In order to accomplish that, we need to flatten the curve and stop the spread, allowing us to reset. How long will that take?

We're not going to have answers until some time passes—until we test more, until the outcomes of cases are made certain. But we can certainly construct the formulas that should allow us to calculate possible outcomes as new data comes in, and that should allow us to collectively commit to actions directed at certain outcomes. We require a formula from the government. That's the transparency the markets need, that the American people need. And that, at least, should be attainable over the next two weeks.

Stop Pretending Pandemic Politics Are the New Norm

April 1, 2020

"There are no libertarians in a global pandemic." So goes the smug punchline of large-government advocates who point to the necessity of collective action in the face of an unprecedented global crisis. Without government, they say, we'd all be dead.

Few libertarians would disagree. The hardcore libertarians at Reason magazine aren't spending their days fulminating over the evils of government-required lockdown orders in the face of a fast-spreading, deadly disease. That's because they, like all other sentient human beings, recognize that collective action is sometimes necessary.

But here's the dirty little secret: Institutional failures during this pandemic are more indicative of what our politics should be during nonpandemic situations, not the blunt-force ability of the government to shut down the global economy and force us all to stay home. The question isn't whether government has power. Government *is* power. The question is how and when to apply that power. And what we've seen is that government sucks at everything, even the most basic things it is supposed to do well.

Democrats and the media like to pretend that government's failures in this process aren't endemic to government control. They like to blame such failures on Republicans, and on President Donald Trump specifically. But that's just not the case. Human beings are fallible, stupid, gullible and self-interested. Human beings who have the power of government to back them are not less human for having that power. Their humanity just has direr consequences, which is why in nonemergency circumstances, checks and balances are absolutely necessary.

Take, for example, the early days of the pandemic. Democrats say Trump was slow to respond to the incipient threat. But so were Democrats. House Speaker Nancy Pelosi recently declared, "As Trump fiddles, people are dying," but in late February, she was walking the streets of Chinatown, encouraging citizens to join her. New York Mayor Bill De Blasio has ripped Trump for his supposed downplaying of the virus, but De Blasio spent a month poo-pooing its threat. When confronted about that simple fact by CNN's Jake Tapper, De Blasio conveniently suggested that stop looking backward.

Why should we trust these people, exactly?

Or take the roots of America's inability to provide the health care resources necessary to hospitals across the country. While state and local governments were frittering away billions of dollars on useless government spending, they did precisely nothing to prepare for exactly the sort of black swan events for which governments were presumably invented. The Centers for Disease Control and Prevention spent a month failing to produce useful tests and prevented physicians in Seattle from performing proper testing, even after President Trump issued a travel ban on China. For years in advance, members of the federal government of both parties had been warned about the need for ventilators and masks. No one produced or stockpiled them. The Food and Drug Administration's red tape prevented the quick development of new measures to deal with the novel coronavirus.

Why should these people control our lives, when the threat of the red death isn't hovering on our doorstep?

The government is a giant, lumbering idiot. Sometimes we need a giant, lumbering idiot. Almost always, we do not. And those who have used this pandemic response—one of the rare times we need a giant, lumbering idiot to intimidate people into preventing mass infection of one another, and to borrow the money necessary to redress the injuries thus incurred—as a rationale for a government-run "new politics" should have their heads examined.

The 3 Big Questions Nobody Is Answering

April 8, 2020

This week, according to members of the federal government, and state and local governments, Americans have begun to flatten the curve in the novel coronavirus outbreak. The excitement was muted— after all, trends can easily reverse—but real. Americans have abided by recommendations and orders. They've left their jobs to stay at home; they've practiced social distancing; in many places, they've donned masks. The result: a reduction in expected hospitalization and death. According to the University of Washington Institute for Health Metrics and Evaluation model most oft cited by members of the Trump administration, the expected need for hospital beds at peak outbreak was revised down by over 120,000, the number of ventilators by nearly 13,000 and the number of overall deaths by August by nearly 12,000.

Here's the problem: We still don't know the answers to the key questions that will allow the economy to reopen.

First, what is the true coronavirus fatality rate? This question is important because it determines whether certain areas ought to be open or closed, whether we ought to pursue—Sweden style—a more liberalized society that presumes wide spread, or whether we ought to lock down further.

We've seen case fatality rates—the number of deaths divided by the number of identified COVID-19 cases—but both the numerator and the denominator are likely wrong. We don't know how many people have actually died of coronavirus. Some sources suggest the number has been overestimated, given that classification for cause of death, particularly among elderly patients, can be variable. Some sources suggest the number is dramatically underestimated, since many people are dying at home.

Even more importantly, we have no clue how many Americans actually have coronavirus. Some scientists suggest that the number of identified cases could be an order of magnitude lower than the number of people who have had coronavirus and not been tested. That would mean that the fatality rate is actually far lower than suggested, even if the transmission rate is high.

Secondly, what are we expecting in terms of a second wave? The institute's model simply cuts off in early August. It does not predict how many people will die in a second wave. This is the most important problem because experts maintain that the virus is seasonal, which means we are likely to see more serious spreading in the fall. And *that* means we will be faced with either renewed lockdowns for large swaths of the population, with wide-scale testing and contact tracing, or with the realization that we will have to isolate those who are most vulnerable and let everyone else work.

Which raises the third question: What exactly *can* we do? Are we capable of rolling out tens of millions of tests over the next few months—and compelling people to take tests regularly, since the virus is transmittable while carriers are asymptomatic? Can we create a contact tracing system for 330 million Americans—and are we willing to submit ourselves to one?

One thing is certain: Things cannot continue as they have been. Americans are not going to stay home for months on end, and they certainly will not do so on the basis of ever-evolving models, especially as statistics roll in that look like the lower-end model estimates in terms of death and the upper-end estimates in terms of economic damage. We need transparency and honesty from our scientific experts—we need to know what they know, what they don't and when they hope to know what they don't. We're grown-ups, and we're willing to follow their advice. But they need to start answering serious questions, or they will fall prey to the same lack of institutional faith to which all other American institutions seem deeply prone.

What Does Reopening Look Like?

April 15, 2020

As our national lockdown drags on, Americans seem less and less inclined to move swiftly toward societal reopening. Perhaps that's due to the consistent media focus on the risks of reopening. Perhaps that's also due to the psychological comfort of the status quo: When we've been made to feel safe in our home, it's difficult to leave it. Or perhaps we, as a society, have so fundamentally altered our own perception of risk aversion that we aren't willing to leave our houses unless the risk is close to zero.

Whatever the reason, it is simply untenable to lock Americans down for months more. Calls to do so ignore not only the catastrophic human suffering inflicted on millions—employees who no longer have jobs, children who can no longer attend school, entrepreneurs who have seen their life's dreams and savings destroyed at the behest of the government—but the reality of economics, which is that government cannot interminably pay everyone to stay at home. Furthermore, long-term lockdowns do not even prevent the virus from eventual second-wave spreading; when we emerge from our homes, we will pass the virus to one another again.

So, how should we view the risks of reopening our society?

Rationally.

This means that we should stop looking at false case fatality rates as inevitabilities. We simply don't know how many Americans have had coronavirus, or how many have it now. We *do* know that the number of confirmed cases is far lower than the number of cases in society more broadly. In New York, the supposed case fatality rate—the number of deaths from coronavirus over the number of confirmed cases—rests at around 5%. But between March 22 and April 4, 215 pregnant women were screened for COVID-19 in New York City, according to The New England Journal of Medicine. Four women had symptoms of COVID-19, and 29 tested positive despite being asymptomatic. This means 13.7% of these women had COVID-19 without knowing it—for every symptomatic woman, there were seven others who were asymptomatic but positive. If applied statewide—a simplistic model but certainly one that would be closer to accuracy than mere confirmed cases—this would drop the case fatality rate from 5% to 0.7%. Needless to say, such a statistic would alleviate some worry, particularly among less vulnerable populations.

We should also stop treating all cohorts of American society as equally vulnerable to coronavirus. According to two New York University studies, the first most predictive condition for hospitalization was age: Almost half of all coronavirus patients hospitalized in New York City were over the age of 65. The next most predictive condition was obesity. And over 70% of hospitalized coronavirus patients had a chronic condition. This should be no surprise: As of April 12, the New York City Health Department reported 128 fatalities among people with no underlying conditions and just 26 deaths among people below age 45 with no underlying conditions. There were 42,524 diagnosed cases of COVID-19 for New Yorkers under age 45, meaning that the case fatality rate—again, a seriously high-end estimate given the fact that asymptomatic people have not been tested—for those with no underlying health conditions below age 45 is 0.06%. In other words, 9,994 out of every 10,000 young, healthy people who get coronavirus will not die—and the number is likely higher than that.

This means that we should be looking to send young, healthy people back to work, and urging social distancing and isolation for those who are elderly or have preexisting conditions that raise coronavirus risks. We should retain social distancing for the young and healthy, urge mask wearing and perform contact tracing when hot spots arise. We should continue to avoid large-scale gatherings. We should urge special vigilance in high-density areas. Localism is our friend here. But there is a path toward reopening. To ignore it isn't just foolish; it's counterproductive.

Every Crisis an Opportunity

April 22, 2020

This week, the price of oil futures collapsed catastrophically. In fact, the prices collapsed into negative territory in the near term. This bizarre situation, prompted by lack of consumer demand and lack of storage facility, led the irrepressible Rep. Alexandria Ocasio-Cortez, D-N.Y., to tweet: "You absolutely love to see it. This along with record low interest rates means it's the right time for a worker-led, mass investment in green infrastructure to save our planet." This tweet was too dumb even for her—an extraordinary bar, given her past commentary—and she deleted it. But she then reiterated the point in a follow-up tweet, characterizing the rock-bottom oil prices as a "key opportunity" to "create millions of jobs transitioning to renewable and clean energy."

Needless to say, investing in expensive green energy at a time when oil producers cannot *give away oil* is peak stupidity. But the Boston University economics major's faux pas merely underscores an uncomfortable truth regarding this pandemic and its aftermath: For the most partisan, every crisis is an opportunity to push political priors.

The most obvious agenda item for those on the political left has been the growth of government. Dan Balz, chief correspondent of The Washington Post, drooled while saying: "For the first time, many Americans are looking to government for their very economic survival. In time, that could make them look at government differently." Sen. Bernie Sanders, I-Vt., wrote for The New York Times that the "unequal impact of the pandemic and economic collapse are forcing us to rethink the assumptions of our system." Among those assumptions: the free market economy (Sanders terms the free market "the path of greed and unfettered capitalism"). The New York Times termed the coronavirus a "new frontier in the fight for civil rights" and quoted race hustler the Rev. Jesse Jackson, who is calling for a government commission to investigate the "racism and discrimination built into public policies" that result in racial health disparities.

Precisely this attitude—that every crisis is a new weapon in the war for more expansive government, and in favor of a complete rethinking of the constitutional bargain—will lead more and more Americans to view shutdown orders with skepticism. It is one thing to lock down populations on a bipartisan basis with clear goals—goals like preventing coronavirus patients from swamping the health care system. Most Americans will go along with that, and most Americans are willing to grant policymakers the benefit of the doubt.

But when politicians begin to reveal ulterior motives for such shutdowns, Americans begin to ask questions. When politicians simultaneously take measures that obviously do nothing to combat the coronavirus—measures like locking public parks where people are social distancing, or banning Americans from buying gardening supplies but ensuring access to abortion remains fully available— Americans begin to wonder whether their politicians are trustworthy. And when politicians meet such questions with hysterical accusations that the questioners simply don't care about human life, Americans grow even more suspicious.

Crises require trust in authority. But authorities must earn our trust with well-founded, sensible policy. They must be transparent about what they are doing and why they are doing it. When authorities instead suggest openly that their agenda isn't solely curbing the coronavirus but remaking America along the lines of their own political priors, they lose our trust. And they should.

The Biden Double Standard

April 29, 2020

This week, new evidence emerged in the sexual assault allegation by former Joe Biden staffer Tara Reade against the presumptive 2020 Democratic presidential nominee. According to Business Insider, four people have stated that Reade told them contemporaneously about her accusation that Biden forcibly penetrated her with his fingers in 1993. Meanwhile, the Media Research Center uncovered a clip, purportedly of Reade's mother, calling into "Larry King Live" back in 1993 to obliquely refer to the allegation. While such evidence does not speak to the actual event at issue, it does demonstrate that Reade has been talking about the alleged incident since it occurred.

The media ignored the original allegation for weeks. Now, even while reporting on the new developments, they've found ways to downplay their importance. Thus, The Washington Post—democracy dies in darkness!—wrote an article headlined "Trump allies highlight new claims regarding allegations against Biden." Normally, headlines are designed to convey information about the underlying story. This headline was apparently written in English, translated to Swahili and then to Punjabi via Google Translate and then back to English before printing.

Other news outlets skipped the revelations altogether. The New York Times, which ran a comprehensive piece two weeks ago attempting to debunk Reade's case, completely ignored the new information. NBC News didn't bother covering the information either. Meanwhile, NBC News and MSNBC Chairman Andy Lack printed a piece on the network website celebrating its journalistic performance. "Humbled by the responsibility we bear, we try our damnedest to serve our audience," he said. It's a wonder Lack didn't dislocate both arms trying desperately to pat himself on the back.

As of this writing, Biden has not been asked a single direct question about Reade by a television reporter. Meanwhile, members of the media cheer their audacity in asking President Donald Trump questions like, "If an American president loses more Americans over the course of six weeks than died in the entirety of the Vietnam War, does he deserve to be reelected?" So. Much. Journalisming.

Why does any of this matter? Not because Biden should be convicted in the court of public opinion without evidence. He shouldn't. The standards of due process should apply evenly, regardless of partisanship. Supreme Court Justice Brett Kavanaugh should not have been subjected to thousands of hit pieces, magazine covers and twisted accusations that his anger at rape accusations he disputed was mere evidence of his privilege. Christine Blasey Ford should not have been celebrated nationwide as a symbol of truth telling without any corroborative evidence. #BelieveAllWomen was always an idiotic slogan. Only now are members of the media admitting it.

That's why this matters. Biden's candidacy will survive Tara Reade: Democrats aren't dumping Biden overboard based on a 27-year-old accusation of questionable veracity, and they certainly won't do so when running against Trump, who has his own checkered history. But the media's pathetically hypocritical standard on due process and sexual assault allegations won't survive. Neither will their credibility. President Trump spends an inordinate amount of time bashing the media for their lack of seriousness. The same media who laureled Democrats for cashiering Kavanaugh and now spend their days studiously avoiding any talk about Tara Reade deserve every ounce of skepticism the American people can muster.

There's a serio-comic tenor to this whole situation. We're living in a time when we must trust the media more than ever—to bring us unbiased, factual information about a global pandemic, to warn us of dangers and to be reasonable about risk assessment. Yet the media have spent so many years burning through their credibility that they have little left. That's their own fault. If they wish to restore their credibility, they could start by apologizing for their Kavanaugh coverage—and by providing some fact-checking about their own political motivations.

What Are We Trying to Accomplish With Coronavirus Policy?

May 6, 2020

As Americans debate how to reopen our society in the wake of COVID-19, we seem to be breaking down into three groups: first, those who believe the virus isn't particularly serious and desperately want to reopen everything as soon as possible (a small minority of Americans, by polling data); second, those who believe the virus is extraordinarily serious and want everything to remain closed as long as possible (a significant minority of Americans); and third, those who believe the virus is extraordinarily serious, that the economic damage brought about by COVID-19 is extraordinarily serious and that we will have to reopen in considered fashion (the vast majority of Americans). While politicians on either side of the debate hope to position their opponents as advocates of either group 1 or group 2, the reality is that the honest debate is happening within group 3.

So, what does a considered coronavirus reopening strategy look like?

That question rests on a deeper question: What assumptions are we making?

Obviously, we all want to reduce deaths to the lowest possible number. But what assumptions are baked into our policy recommendations? Are we assuming a vaccine will come along in three, six, 12 or 18 months? Are we assuming herd immunity conferred at 60% of the population, or 80%? Are we assuming therapeutic measures that would reduce the infection fatality rates by 20, 30 or 100%, and within what period of time?

We also want to reduce economic harm to the lowest possible level. Again, we must ask what assumptions are baked into our policy recommendations. Are we assuming that a 75% reduction in restaurant seating will save 50% of restaurants? Are we assuming that shoppers will continue to socially distance six months from now? Are we assuming that the government will be able to shoulder trillions more in debt despite an underlying decrease in international appetite for such debt?

The question of assumptions is key to our policymaking. That's because if we assume the worst—no therapeutics that seriously knock down the infection fatality rate, no vaccines for 18 months or more and an economy that simply cannot function at one-quarter or even half of normal capacity—then we are forced to a simple conclusion: In the absence of any significant change to the status quo, we must pursue a strategy of so-called controlled avalanche.

That strategy has been coined by Israeli scientists, who suggest that the best strategy for reducing deaths while achieving herd immunity would be to tranche populations and then expose the least-vulnerable populations to COVID-19 in order to let them develop antibodies—in essence, performing with public health the same function ski resorts perform when they create small avalanches in order to avoid a major avalanche. The simple fact is that 40% to 50%, at low estimate, of all deaths in the European Union from COVID-19 have occurred at nursing homes; the same is true in California. Had the authorities properly protected nursing homes, the infection fatality rate across the industrialized world could be *half* of the current rate.

It is also true that the infection fatality rate for COVID-19 ranges widely by age: As of late April, of the 37,308 deaths recorded by the Centers for Disease Control and Prevention, just 1,036 were people under the age of 45, and just 51 were below the age of 25. Even among younger populations, the vast majority of deaths were people with underlying conditions. Israeli scientists suggest that protecting the elderly and the vulnerable and then allowing herd immunity to develop among the least vulnerable would radically reduce overall mortality (by over 40%), reduce the maximum number of people in need for ICUs (by over 60%) and decrease the time required to allow freedom to low-risk populations by months.

This is obviously not a foolproof strategy—there is no foolproof strategy. But it may be a better strategy than simply hoping for the best while watching the world economy implode, even as we know that our deepest hopes for a deus ex machina may go unrewarded.

How the Obama Administration Shattered the Rule of Law

May 13, 2020

This week, former President Barack Obama reemerged from hibernation to lecture Americans about the threat to rule of law posed by the Trump administration. After Attorney General Bill Barr announced that the Department of Justice would be dropping its case against President Donald Trump's former national security advisor Michael Flynn, who had pled guilty to one count of lying to the FBI, Obama told his former aides, "our basic understanding of rule of law is at risk." He explained, "There is no precedent that anybody can find for someone who has been charged with perjury just getting off scot-free. ... And when you start moving in those directions, it can accelerate pretty quickly as we've seen in other places."

In reality, of course, Flynn was never charged with perjury. He was charged with lying to the FBI in the course of an investigation, a separate and far lesser offense, particularly given the fact that his alleged lie was immaterial to any underlying crime. In fact, as America found out over the past two weeks, Flynn wasn't supposed to be the subject of any investigation at all: The FBI had decided to close an investigation into Flynn in January 2017, even after supposedly nefarious calls between Flynn and Russian Ambassador Sergey Kislyak. Disgraced former FBI agent Peter Strzok—the same man who pledged to lover and former FBI attorney Lisa Page that Donald Trump would never be president and suggested an "insurance policy" against that possibility—then intervened to keep the investigation open. The next day, during an Oval Office meeting, President Obama himself asked then-FBI Director James Comey about the Flynn-Kislyak communications. Next, Comey upped the ante: He avoided following normal FBI-White House protocols in order to interview Flynn, and Comey's deputy director, Andrew McCabe, avoided informing Flynn of his rights. Nonetheless, the FBI agents who conducted the interview suggested that they did not think Flynn was lying during that interview. As it turns out, notes between top FBI officials at the time said, "What's our goal? Truth/Admission or to get him to lie, so we can prosecute him or get him fired?" Flynn would later plead guilty to one count of lying to the FBI—at least in part because the FBI was threatening his son with prosecution.

This should be a massive scandal. It should be a massive scandal because, at the very least, it demonstrates the nation's chief law enforcement agencies, prompted by political actors at the very top of the government, racing to bend the rules in order to pursue a case they were convinced they would make: the case that the Trump campaign had conspired with the Russian government. From the purposefully botched Carter Page Foreign Intelligence Surveillance Act warrant to the absurdly conjured prosecution of Flynn, the most powerful institutions in American life violated the protocols meant to restrict abuse, firmly secure in their own feelings of moral rectitude.

That's the best-case scenario.

The worst-case scenario is far darker: that by early January, with no evidence of Russian collusion, leaders of the nation's political and law enforcement agencies decided that guilt was irrelevant, and that the Trump administration had to be strangled in the crib. This seems like a major stretch, but in a highly partisan era, such a narrative will have legs.

Meanwhile, blithe in the knowledge that they were on the side of the angels, members of the Obama-era government continue to chide Attorney General Bill Barr for ending a charade of a case. Their incredible inability to see how their conduct looks beyond the echo chamber of sycophantic media sources only undermines their credibility further. As it turns out, President Obama isn't wrong—at least not entirely. Our basic understanding of the rule of law is at risk, not because Bill Barr stepped in to prevent an unjust prosecution but because our institutions under the Obama administration were politicized in ways that should shock the American conscience.

How Biden Could Be Handing Trump His Reelection

May 20, 2020

In national polling, former vice president Joe Biden is the clear 2020 front-runner. He's up nearly 5 points in the RealClearPolitics polling average; he's up in Wisconsin, Pennsylvania, Florida and Arizona. That's because Biden campaigned as the anti-Bernie Sanders: a "return to normalcy" candidate rather than a transformational one. His entire pitch relied on his high name recognition, the general perception of his likability and his unthreatening demeanor.

The coronavirus pandemic merely underscored this pitch. Biden hasn't waned in the national polling since the pandemic—his lead has been utterly consistent. That's true even though Biden has been relegated to his basement, gaffing through completely anodyne statements about COVID-19, glitching his way to a few thousand viewers at a time, being interrupted by the birds honking outside his window. How can a major party candidate win if nobody cares whether he's even alive? Because Biden's candidacy isn't a referendum on Biden but on Trump: President Donald Trump is widely perceived as volatile, unstable, chaotic. Biden is perceived as somnambulant. Better a sleepwalker, many voters seem to think, than the rolling chaos of a second Trump term.

Yet somehow, the Biden campaign has decided to abandon Biden's greatest advantage: his promise of a sedated interregnum. Instead, according to The New York Times, Biden's campaign will embrace radical proposals. "With Mr. Biden leading President Trump in the polls, the former vice president and other Democratic leaders are racing to assemble a new governing agenda that meets the extraordinary times—and they agree it must be far bolder than anything the party establishment has embraced before," The Times reported.

Some of the new proposals are directly from the Sanders campaign: forgiving student loans, a Green New Deal, expansion of government health care, a government jobs plan, a ban on stock buybacks and compulsion toward profit sharing for corporations. Meanwhile, former President Barack Obama explained over the weekend that the coronavirus has merely underscored deep-seated American racism that requires a complete remaking of our society. Equating disparate health and incomes between black Americans and white Americans due to COVID-19 with the shooting of black Georgian Ahmaud Arbery—and citing both as legacies of America's historic racism—Obama stated, "No generation has been better positioned to be warriors for justice and remake the world."

But do Americans really want the world remade? Or are they simply longing for the world of four months ago, when unemployment stood at 3.5%, when incomes were rising at the lowest end of the income scale, when Americans could attend events without fear of infection and death? Are Americans truly desperate for a reshaping of our medical system, a universal basic income and trillions more in debt?

Biden seems to be betting on the latter. And that's idiocy of the highest order. It completely undermines his entire case for the nomination; it allows Trump to place the new radical agenda front and center, rather than his own foibles. Biden's go-for-broke strategy is a massive opportunity for Trump—if Trump doesn't blow it.

Making the World a Worse Place, One Twitter Mob at a Time

May 27, 2020

Life is filled with nuance, with complexity. Take, for example, the case of Amy Cooper. Cooper is a 41-year-old white woman who worked at Franklin Templeton, an asset management firm. She was walking her dog without a leash in the Ramble section of Central Park when she was confronted by a black man named Christian Cooper (no relation). He told her to leash her dog; she refused. According to Christian, he then stated, "Look, if you're going to do what you want, I'm going to do what I want, but you're not going to like it." She asked what he meant. He then summoned her dog, planning to give the dog treats. "I pull out the dog treats I carry for just such intransigence," he explained.

At that point, he began filming the exchange. She told him to stop taping; he refused. While grabbing her dog by its collar, she informed him she would call the cops. "I'm going to tell them there's an African American man threatening my life," she said. He responded, "Please tell them whatever you like." She did, in fact, call the police, and said: "I'm in the Ramble, and there's a man, African American. He has a bicycle helmet, and he is recording me and threatening me and my dog."

In real life, we'd examine the issue as objectively as possible. It appears that Christian Cooper did indeed say something vaguely threatening—"I'm going to do what I want, but you're not going to like it"—and then attempted to get her dog to approach him. It also appears that Amy Cooper threatened him in racist fashion, implicitly suggesting that by telling the police that a black man was threatening her life, she could place him in mortal danger.

Suffice it to say that the proper solution here would have been for Amy Cooper to apologize and recognize the implicit racism in her own statements, for Christian Cooper to forgive her and for everyone to move on.

Instead, Christian Cooper posted the video. Twitter went wild. The outcome: Amy was labeled a racist and fired from her job, and had to surrender her dog. Her life was effectively ruined.

The world of social media has not made us any more responsible, any kinder or any more decent. It has made us far worse. That's because Twitter isn't about signaling virtue. It's about signaling *commitment*. It's insufficient to merely analyze events and give an honest take. You must be *for* or *against* something. And you demonstrate full *commitment* to that position. Your entire online identity rests on others retweeting or liking your purity of heart. There is no risk—only reward—in dunking on Amy Cooper, tweeting at her employer, encouraging her destruction. You will be rewarded for your anti-racism, amply demonstrated with just a few clicks. If you suggest any motivational complexity—that perhaps Amy Cooper said something racist and over-the-top but wasn't lying when she said she felt threatened—then you will be tarred as insufficiently committed to the anti-racist cause.

This logic holds across the board. If President Donald Trump sends out a series of bizarre and morally reprehensible tweets accusing Joe Scarborough of murdering a congressional intern—and if you point out that this is both bizarre and morally reprehensible—then you will be labeled insufficiently loyal to the cause. It's not about truth; it's not about decency; it's about signaling your *commitment*.

In the real world, commitment without decency is a sin. Online, commitment without decency is a virtue. Which is why if you spend too much time on Twitter, you probably ought to be committed.

The Controlled Burn Rages out of Control

June 3, 2020

In the wake of riots that have spread across America, leaving shattered businesses and wounded communities in their wake, it feels as though our nation is collapsing around us. That's bizarre, considering that virtually all Americans agree with the following two propositions: first, that it is evil for a police officer to place his knee on the neck of a prone suspect struggling to breathe for eight long minutes; second, that breaking store windows; stealing televisions and shoes; beating business owners; and attacking police officers is wrong. That seeming unanimity should mean unity in the face of police brutality and rioting and looting.

It doesn't.

It doesn't because members of our political class have decided that instead of rallying against obvious evil, Americans must be categorized as enlightened or benighted based on their answer to one question: Was America and is America rooted in racism and bigotry? If you answer in the negative, you are complicit in racism and bigotry, say our media, academic leaders and high-ranking members of the Democratic Party. If you answer in the affirmative, you may be categorized among the woke, the aware, the sensitive and the decent.

This is a nonsensical and dangerous game. But it's a game pressed forward by the most powerful messaging institutions in our society: our media, who award Pulitzer Prizes to *faux* history like The 1619 Project, which argues that every American institution has been fatally corrupted by America's original sin, slavery, and that every inequality of today can find its root in inequities of the past; our celebrities, who proudly proclaim that rights to free speech, property ownership and due process are merely facades for the continuing and malign maintenance of structural inequalities; and too many of our politicians, who casually attribute every instance of police brutality to deep-seated American racism.

These are lies. America's history *is* replete with racism and oppression, but that's because America didn't hold true to her founding ideals; America's philosophy is good and true, and her flaws are thanks to her failures to follow that philosophy. It is a lie to attack Americans' fundamental rights as outgrowths of persecution. And it's a damnable calumny to liken the treatment of black Americans in 2020 to the treatment of black Americans in 1960, let alone 1860. Yet we are told by our institutional elites that to point out these lies is to refuse responsibility, to provide cover for racism.

Declaring America's most fundamental structures corrupt and cancer-ridden is deeply dangerous. Once a structure has been condemned, its foundations declared unstable, it can only be destroyed. There is no way to argue that fealty to a particular political program *inside* that supposedly corrupt structure can fix the problem. Former President Barack Obama, who declares that discrimination exists in "almost every institution of our lives," and that "the legacy of slavery, Jim Crow ... that's still part of our DNA that's passed on," says that voting for local officials is the solution to police brutality and individual instances of racism. Somehow, so long as we vote for the same Democratic politicians who have governed nearly every major American city for decades, America's founding sins can be extirpated. Is anyone expected to believe this? Our elites cannot set fire to the fundamentals of America and then hope to contain that fire to occasional trips to the voting booth.

So Americans are left with a choice. We can either think of one another with charity and accuracy, acknowledging the sins of America's past while recognizing that America remains a beacon of freedom and decency. Or we can continue to follow the path of those who would tear us apart. To follow the latter course isn't sensitive or moral. It places the very existence of our common republic at risk.

Woke Chaos and Naked Power

June 10, 2020

With the death of George Floyd—a heinous atrocity virtually every American decries—unity should have prevailed. Americans hate police brutality; Americans care about black lives; Americans despise looting and rioting; Americans want to protect citizens but preserve the ability of the police to stop crime.

Instead, the country seems to be falling apart. That's because of the utterly chaotic political and media response to the Floyd tragedy: a response that demands agreement but, most of all, requires compliance. You must kneel.

You must kneel because you cannot understand. You simply cannot. If you have to ask for a definition of systemic privilege, we are told, it's because your white privilege has blinded you to reality. If you point out that not all inequality is inequity, we are told, it is because your latent racism is leeching into your worldview. If you defend America's history, philosophy and culture—or, God forbid, her flag—you must apologize. And, if Drew Brees is any indicator, your wife must also apologize, and your second cousin once removed.

You may not understand what is being demanded of you. You may see the wave of conflicting messages emanating from the press and wonder just what you're supposed to do. But the chaos is the point. You are *supposed* to be confused. Confusion is a political weapon. Clarity is a shield. If our media and political class can prevent clarity, they can prevent unity; if they can obscure, they can demand acquiescence.

Thus, we hear messages that are obviously in direct conflict with one another. And, we are told, our inability to square those messages means that we must listen to the woke priesthood that can untangle these Gordian knots.

Thus, we hear that silence is violence, that being non-racist simply isn't enough and you must actively fight racism. But we also hear that speech is violence, that if you oppose policies the political left supports, your words are a form of violence and you must be silenced. The only safe path, therefore, is parroting the messages of those initiated in the religion of wokeness.

Thus, we hear that individuals ought not be held responsible for the sins of those in their racial group, and that's why it's so wrong for police to engage in profiling. But we also hear that white Americans bear full responsibility for the sins of both modern racists and historic racists, and ought to atone on behalf of their race and their country. And if you refuse, you must be considered racist.

Thus, we hear that the police are the greatest threat to black Americans, and that's why they must be defunded. But we also hear that police absence, a product of racism, created the conditions that originally led to higher crime rates in black communities. We can, therefore, blame the police for crime whether they're present or absent in minority communities.

Thus, we hear that the rioting and looting were exaggerated by the media, or that they were largely the product of white antifa members. But we also hear that rioting and looting are the justified outgrowth of centuries of black rage. You cannot, therefore, oppose rioting and looting too strenuously, lest you be labeled a racist.

Thus, we hear that COVID-19 is so extraordinarily dangerous that anti-lockdown protesters were endangering the lives of other Americans; in fact, they were racist, since COVID-19 has disproportionately affected minority communities. But we also hear that protesting racism is so extraordinarily important that we can freely ignore all restrictions surrounding COVID-19—and, indeed, that we have an obligation to do so.

Thus, we hear that journalists ought to be treated with the utmost respect because they are doing a difficult job and pursuing facts and the truth; and that harsh words spoken about journalists reflect underlying unease about freedom of the press. But we also hear that journalists are actually activists and thus have a duty *not* to be objective; op-ed editors should be fired for the sin of greenlighting pieces opposed by woke staffers.

In the end, our republic runs only so long as we're able to hold some semblance of logical conversation with one another. But the republic isn't running. Instead, we are battered with logically incoherent nonsense, a variety of messages that carry only one consistent bottom line: Shut up. Believe. Repeat. The chaos of the moment isn't a bug; it's a feature. And the more confused we are, the less we can possibly hold together, despite the fact that nearly all Americans agree on the most important issues.

Our Totalitarian Moment

June 17, 2020

America feels like it's falling apart.

That's because it is.

There are two ways to achieve unity in any group. The first is to set up a few serious standards of conduct, policed with the absolute minimum of compulsion, and then allow freedom in all other matters. This was the founding vision for our federal government. In this vision, we agree not to infringe upon one another's life, liberty and property, and we create a government capable of preventing or prosecuting such infringements. Then, so long as we abide by those simple standards, we are free to pursue our own paths. Diverse ways of life can coexist within this broader group membership. Governance becomes largely a matter of localism—places with homogenous values setting further standards for *their* group membership. But our broadest-group membership is easy to obtain and easy to maintain.

The founding vision for unity presupposed a flawed human nature: People were capable of sin individually but capable of the greatest sin when backed with the power of federal force. The founding vision for unity also presupposed an agreement on the nature of rights and liberty: No man had a right to demand anything from his neighbor. Furthermore, the founding vision for unity presupposed that our strongest bonds would exist outside of government—in our families, our communities, our churches.

The founding vision has now been abandoned in pursuit of something more *fulfilling*: a communitarian vision of reality in which the will of the mob is perceived as virtuous; in which every man has the right to protect himself from the vicissitudes of life and the cruelties of history by demanding redress from his neighbors; in which our strongest bonds are forged at the most centralized level.

This second path toward unity requires purification. This path seeks homogeneity in place of diversity, top-down standards in place of localism. Standards for membership are not weak or broad—membership cannot be obtained simply by avoiding encroaching on others' life, liberty or property. Membership can only be obtained and maintained through strict compliance with an increasingly arcane set of rules and standards. Politically, this means a demanding legal regime with heavy coercion. Culturally, this means braying mobs of ideological enforcers, casting out unbelievers into the cornfields.

This second model of governance is promoted by the political left today. In this view, diversity of viewpoint cannot be allowed; unity of viewpoint in all things is the predicate for all serious change. Once the group has been purified, change will require only the snap of a finger. No more gridlock; no more conversation. The collective can be activated quickly and powerfully.

This second model of governance is totalitarian in nature, and it is toward that model we are now moving as a society. Politically, those who deny that the collective ought to have the power to override individual rights must be punished; culturally, they must be exiled. They must be deemed unworthy. To stand up for individual rights in this climate means to be labeled a defender of privilege. To deny the systemic evil of the United States means to betray your moral unworthiness.

The great irony is that the second model of unity—the totalitarian purification rituals we watch before us—will never achieve unity. It will achieve further division, as more and more people fall short of ideological purity, or refuse to bow before the ideological demands of the perpetual revolutionaries.

We could agree to live with one another, as individuals under the broader rubric of rights. If we don't, we won't be living with one another at all.

The Only Good People in History

June 24, 2020

Truly, we live in auspicious times.

Those who have sinned will be cast down; those who are sinless will set new social standards for the rest of us. After all, we now live in the only generation ever to produce truly virtuous human beings.

What else should we make of the graceless religious wokeness promoted by our moral betters, such immaculate moral personages as Robin DiAngelo, author of "White Fragility," and Nikole Hannah-Jones, Pulitzer Prize-winning creator of The New York Times' pseudo-historical 1619 Project? DiAngelo informs us that all white people are sinners by nature, inculcated in the evils of whiteness and utterly incapable of repenting such sin ... unless, of course, they purchase a diversity training course. DiAngelo says that it isn't enough to oppose racism: we must "interrupt" the systems in which we live in order to become "anti-racist," a vaguely defined term apparently meaning nothing so much as parroting the more purple writings of Ibram X. Kendi.

Hannah-Jones, meanwhile, happily takes credit for the rioting and looting that has wracked the country and that she has spent time justifying—she recently thanked a critic online for terming this unrest "the 1619 riots." Furthermore, we are informed by this arbiter of the great and the good that we must never say that figures like Ulysses S. Grant—a man who wrecked the Confederacy and devastated the Ku Klux Klan but also held one of his wife's slaves in bondage before freeing him—were "men of their times." After all, "Hitler was a man of his time. Osama bin Laden was a man of his time," she said in a now-deleted tweet.

We, however, live in an age of true heroes—people who live outside of time; people of sterling quality who need no context, require no nuance and brook no dissent. All who stand before them must bow or be canceled. Old tweets will be resurfaced; old comedy sketches will be censored. All those who came before were complicit in the system, and thus, must pay.

So young woke leftists cheer as they tear down monuments of George Washington and Thomas Jefferson; Generation Z college students chide their parents and grandparents—many of whom, in minority communities, experienced actual discrimination and hardship—as insufficiently committed to the cause of anti-racism. Gisselle Quintero, 18, told The Washington Post about her grandparents. "(T)hey were prohibited from drinking at 'whites-only' fountains after long, hot days of working in the fields," The Post wrote, and "tried to distinguish themselves by their hard work and achievement." But, clearly because they lacked enthusiasm for the current woke revolution, "They just kind of suppressed those memories." Quintero's grandparents may have overcome actual racism, but she posted news of a protest at a local mall on her social media.

Perhaps we have truly reached the apex of humanity. Or perhaps we are living in a particularly arrogant and self-serving moment when dissociation from America's history and from other Americans substitutes for actual decency; when canceling others is the point, not a means to an end; when joining the woke mob isn't about building something better but merely signaling your own saintliness. Perhaps in reality, those who pull down statues of Washington and Jefferson have accomplished little other than feeling special at the expense of the most special country in human history, and at the expense of their fellow citizens.

The Problem of 'Anti-Racism'

July 1, 2020

Today, the nostrum goes, it is not enough for Americans to be not racist. They must be "anti-racist." This woke terminology has infused our lexicon. Sen. Elizabeth Warren, D-Mass., recently declared from the well of the Senate: "Being race-conscious is not enough. It never was. We must be anti-racists." What, pray tell, is the difference between being against racism and being anti-racist? Ibram X. Kendi, author of "How to Be An Antiracist," provides an answer: Racism is no longer to be defined as the belief that someone is inferior based on race. Instead, racism is to be defined as the belief that *any* group differences can be attributed to *anything other than racism* . Thus, any system that ends with different outcomes must be racist. Indeed, Kendi contends, "Racism itself is institutional, structural, and systemic."

To be anti-racist means to tear down these systems. Any obstacle in the pursuit of equality of outcome must be torn down, assumed to be a product of discrimination. Basic decency, then, means that we must oppose even institutions that have been considered hallmarks of freedom. Those institutions, after all, have exacerbated inequalities, or at least failed to rectify those inequalities.

This means that America's culture of rights—a culture that suggests an obligation on the part of individuals to respect the rights of others, even if they disagree—must come under fire. That culture reinforces hierarchies and inequalities, after all. The classical liberal says that rights fall equally on the just and the unjust alike; the anti-racist suggests that rights are merely tools of power. Anti-racism, in its essence, is merely reworked neo-Marxism from the 1960s: Herbert Marcuse would have been ecstatic to see his concept of "repressive tolerance"—"intolerance against movements from the Right and toleration of movements from the Left"—revived under the banner of race rather than class.

The self-proclaimed "anti-racist" left—a left that sees all of human relations reduced to a rudimentary correlation of skin color and inequality, an analysis we used to call racist—has decided that the culture must be cleansed of all of those who will not be drafted into its woke army. Its march through the institutions began with college campuses, where cowardly administrators quickly caved to the bizarre notion that campuses were unsafe, cruel bastions of bigotry requiring speech codes and training in microaggressions. Next, the woke army moved on to the halls of institutional media, where editors were forced to announce their own white privileges along with their resignations, turning over the instruments of informational dissemination to radical racialists.

Now the woke army has targeted corporations. Corporations are, by nature, risk-averse; they seek merely profit and lack of controversy. The hard left has targeted them as the weakest link in the chain of free speech: If corporations can be bullied into pulling their money from social media networks, those social media networks can be bullied into restricting their free-speech cultures. Remove advertising bucks from Instagram and watch as Instagram censors those the woke want censored.

Indeed, such a campaign is now front and center in the culture wars: Major corporations from Coca-Cola to Target have stopped advertising on social media networks, citing the need for more "hate speech" regulation on those platforms. Obviously, those who target corporations will not be satisfied until all non-woke speech is limited or banned; corporations will be unpleasantly surprised when those they have been seeking to appease turn on them as remnants of the evil system. But corporations have neither the principle nor the will to deny the demands of the loudest and the most militant.

The product of the woke crusade will not be a less racist America but a more polarized one. That's because the woke crusade is not truly about reducing racism; it is about attacking fundamental institutions, American history and our very culture of rights. All the things we share must be eviscerated. So we will share nothing. And then the true ugliness begins.

Not All Black Lives Matter to Black Lives Matter

July 8, 2020

This week, CNN's Don Lemon, who has spent the last few weeks bashing the supposed thoroughgoing systemic racism of the United States, hosted black actor Terry Crews. He then proceeded to browbeat Crews, who had committed the great sin of tweeting, "#ALLBLACKLIVESMATTER 9 black CHILDREN killed by violence in Chicago since June 20, 2020." Lemon specifically objected to Crews' hashtag. After Lemon humbly informed Crews that he has skin "as tough as an armadillo," he then lectured: "The Black Lives Matter movement was started because it was talking about police brutality. ... But that's not what Black Lives Matter is about. It's not ... all-encompassing ... The Black Lives Matter movement is about police brutality and injustice in that matter, not about what's happening in black neighborhoods."

This, of course, is largely false. The Black Lives Matter movement did indeed begin with protests about police brutality but quickly morphed into broader debates over the validity of looting and rioting, tearing down historic statues, slavery reparations and defunding the police. And Black Lives Matter, as Crews correctly pointed out, has never restricted its mandate to the question of police violence: It has announced that its focuses also include police brutality, transgender rights, gay rights, disrupting the nuclear family and freeing Palestine, among other diverse topics.

So why is Lemon so deeply invested in *preventing* conversations about black lives? Why, in fact, do only some black lives matter, rather than all?

That's not merely a question asked by conservatives or contrarians. It's being asked all over the United States by black Americans being left to the predations of criminals, in large part thanks to the woke virtue signaling of many Black Lives Matter leaders and media allies. In Washington, D.C., Mayor Muriel Bowser emblazoned the enormous yellow words "BLACK LIVES MATTER" on 16th Street. Protesters quickly added "DEFUND THE POLICE." One month later, 11-year-old Davon McNeal was shot in the head while heading to a family cookout on July 4. His grandfather, John Ayala, lamented: "We're protesting for months, for weeks, saying, 'Black Lives Matter. Black Lives Matter.' Black lives matter it seems like, only when a police officer shoots a black person. What about all the black-on-black crime that's happening in the community?"

McNeal was just one of the latest victims of a wave of violence gripping America's major cities. Last weekend, at least 89 people were shot in Chicago, leaving at least 17 dead. Shootings in Philadelphia have spiked 67%. In the first week of June, Los Angeles saw a shocking 250% increase in murders from the prior week. New York City's shootings have skyrocketed 44% over last year's numbers; every person shot there the week of June 29—101—was from a minority community. It turns out that the agenda of Black Lives Matter, which includes fighting against the prevalence of police—a call taken up by Democratic mayors and city councils around the United States—endangers black lives far more than the presence of police.

Yet these lives don't particularly matter for Black Lives Matter advocates, apparently. Black lives matter when we're talking about police brutality. But Don Lemon has no airtime each night for those who seek to talk about threats to black lives that dwarf in severity problems related to policing—and that are just as newsworthy. Indeed, the statistical case is unassailable that the daily murder of minority youths in America's major cities is far *more* newsworthy than the latest cable panel discussion of "white fragility" or the "power of whiteness."

But our current Black Lives Matter moment isn't about Davon McNeal, even if the wages of Black Lives Matter's recommended policies are death for those left unprotected by law enforcement. All that matters for too many in our elite institutions is the narrative that

America's systems are the greatest obstacle to black Americans. And not all lives lost are equally valuable in promoting that perverse narrative.

Safety Lies Only in Surrender ... or Resistance

July 15, 2020

This week, gadfly New York Times columnist Bari Weiss resigned her position at the so-called newspaper of record. She did so after years of fielding slings and arrows from her own colleagues and editors, who treated her as an ultra-conservative enemy—this despite the fact that her perspective on the world is an eclectic mix of social progressivism, skepticism toward regulation and foreign policy hawkishness. (Personal disclosure: I, along with many people right, left and center consider Bari a friend.) The pressure on Weiss from within the newspaper had reached extraordinary proportions: Excerpts of staff Slack chats revealed colleagues openly discussing why Weiss ought to lose her job, maligning her as a bigot and suggesting publicly that she is a liar.

So Weiss quit, and she burned the bridge behind her.

"The lessons that ought to have followed the election—lessons about the importance of understanding other Americans, the necessity of resisting tribalism, and the centrality of the free exchange of ideas to a democratic society—have not been learned," Weiss wrote in her resignation letter. "Instead, a new consensus has emerged in the press, but perhaps especially at this paper: that truth isn't a process of collective discovery, but an orthodoxy already known to an enlightened few whose job is to inform everyone else."

This is the nature of the game: Mirror the perspectives of de facto Times editor Nikole Hannah-Jones and her woke colleagues, or find yourself ostracized, publicly shamed and pressured to leave. And the actual editors of The Times have caved to this nonsense time and again. As Weiss raged: "If a person's ideology is in keeping with the new orthodoxy, they and their work remain unscrutinized. Everyone else lives in fear of the digital thunderdome."

Weiss is hardly the exception inside the bastions of leftist groupthink. At Vox.com, co-founder Matthew Yglesias was shamed into silence for suggesting—sin of sins!—that cancel culture is wrong. His co-founder, Ezra Klein, subtweeted Yglesias, even as Yglesias remained quiet. At Princeton University, professor Joshua Katz wrote an open letter decrying demands from fellow Princeton faculty that the university engage in open racial discrimination in favor of minorities. He was quickly labeled a threat to decency, with fellow professor Eddie Glaude complaining, "Professor Katz, at times in this letter, seems to not regard people like me as essential features, or persons, of Princeton."

The list goes on. And on and on.

In fact, there is only one way to avoid the blacklist: to surrender, utterly and completely. Any sign of remaining dissent must be purged. Bow before Zod, or pay the price. Thus, Ben Howe (again—personal disclosure—a friend), an anti-Trump Republican who edited videos for the pro-Joe Biden Lincoln Project, found himself fired from the project for two- and four-year-old tweets. Thus, Gary Garrels, senior curator of painting and sculpture at the San Francisco Museum of Modern Art, was forced to resign his position after he insisted that the museum continue to acquire the odd piece from white artists. The mildest sign of unwillingness to become an "ally" in the Great Culture Purge of 2020 ends with your neck in the guillotine.

Have we finally reached the glorious age in which Absolute Truth is known with such fulsome certainty that our cultural betters should be trusted to wish dissenters away into the cornfield? Of course not. We're just watching the latest cultural revolution in real time. Which leaves those who wish to not be purged with two simple choices: Stand up together against this round of Maoist purification, or hang separately.

America Is Hitting the
Self-Destruct Button

July 22, 2020

On Tuesday, The Wall Street Journal released the results of a poll performed in conjunction with NBC News. The poll found that 56% of Americans believe American society is racist. Seventy-one percent believe race relations are either very or fairly bad. Most troubling, 65% of black Americans say that racial discrimination is built into American society, "including into our policies and institutions."

The notion that America is systemically racist bodes ill for the future. It's also a dramatic lie. American history is replete with racism; racism was indeed the root of systems ranging from slavery to Jim Crow. But the story of America is the story of the cashing of Martin Luther King Jr.'s promissory note: the fulfillment of the pledge of the Declaration of Independence to treat all men equally, to grant them protection of their unalienable natural rights. America has worked to extirpate the nearly universal sin of bigotry in pursuit of the fulfillment of the declaration. The story of America is 1776, not 1619; it's Abraham Lincoln, not John C. Calhoun; it's Martin Luther King Jr., not Robin DiAngelo.

It is particularly true today that American society does not deserve the scorn being heaped upon her head. American society is decidedly *not* racist: According to Swedish economists from World Values, America is one of the most racially tolerant countries on Earth. American law has banned discrimination on race for two generations and more than half a century; in fact, the only racially discriminatory laws on the books cut in favor of racial minorities, who have been granted special privileges in arenas like college admissions.

The police are no longer instruments of racial terror, contrary to popular media narrative: In many of America's largest cities, police forces are either majority minority or nearly so, and police are not more likely to shoot and kill black Americans than white Americans. Problems of high crime in minority neighborhoods are generally a result of *underpolicing*, rather than the converse.

Some problems of wealth inequality are in part products of history—history always has consequences. But overwhelmingly, the pathways to success are not barred by discrimination. Black Americans occupy many of the most prominent positions in American society, from government to entertainment to education to finance. Responsible individual decision-making *is* generally rewarded for all Americans, black and white. And Americans are more than willing to fight those who would obstruct the possibility of success for those who make the right decisions.

More and more Americans apparently believe that the American system is endemically racist—yet the system produces more wealth, freedom and opportunity than any on Earth for millions of citizens of every color, creed and religion. If a majority of Americans believe that society is racist—not just individuals but a vast swath of friends and neighbors, and America's institutions to boot—then it will be quite difficult for Americans to unify. No country can survive its citizens seeing one another as enemies rather than friends, seeing their country as a reflection of continuing evil embedded in its history. America, like every other nation, requires a common philosophy, culture and history to survive. And yet those elements are being consistently eroded by those who would rather collapse the American system in pursuit of some unspecified utopia.

That utopia will not come. All that will follow in the wake of the dissolution of our common bonds is chaos. The principles of the Declaration of Independence remain true; the promise remains durable. The only question is whether we are willing to stand up for those principles and work anew to fulfill those promises, rather than caving in the foundations of the greatest nation ever conceived by mankind.

The Left's Willingness to Tolerate Violence Should Frighten All Americans

July 29, 2020

"Mostly peaceful."

So goes the characterization of demonstrations that have routinely turned into looting and rioting for months on end, from Portland to Seattle to New York to Los Angeles. "Protesters in California set fire to a courthouse, damaged a police station and assaulted officers after a peaceful demonstration intensified," read one recent ABC News tweet. CNN called protests in Portland "mostly peaceful," adding that "they have at times devolved into violence, vandalism, and arson." During riots in Los Angeles in June, as the entire county locked down, the Los Angeles Times noted, "The third night of countywide curfews followed days of massive, mostly peaceful protests ... Nearly 1,200 people were arrested Sunday after police officers clashed with demonstrators and looters shattered windows and emptied stores in Santa Monica and Long Beach."

The phrase "mostly peaceful," then, is rather fungible. Consider that during the tea party protests of 2011, then-Vice President Joe Biden reportedly likened tea partiers to "terrorists"—and those protests were notable mostly for people cleaning up their own litter. When anti-lockdown protesters descended on the Michigan state capitol, a columnist for The New York Times labeled them "armed rebels," despite a complete lack of violence. When three white supremacists were arrested for plotting violence at a pro-gun rally, GQ's Talia Lavin headlined, "That Pro-Gun Rally in Virginia Wasn't Exactly 'Peaceful'"—even though the rally saw no violence.

In truth, the category of "mostly peaceful" is a brand-new invention meant to obscure the simple fact that many of our cultural elites are fine with violence so long as those who engage in such violence have the proper goals. Nikole Hannah-Jones, creator of the pseudo-historical 1619 Project, celebrated when critics labeled rioting and looting "the 1619 riots"; she added that destruction of property was "not violence." This week, Democrats grilling Attorney General Bill Barr could not be bothered to condemn violence, prompting Barr to rant, "What makes me concerned for the country is this is the first time in my memory the leaders of one of our great two political parties, the Democratic Party, are not coming out and condemning mob violence and the attack on federal courts." This should come as little surprise, given that those same cultural elites have cheered on massive protests in a time of a deadly pandemic, explaining that sometimes politics is just too important to stop a raging disease.

Our journey back to the 1960s is nearly complete. Too many Americans have rejected some of the key lessons of that time—that a breakdown in law and order costs lives, that political change does not require violence—in favor of a newfound sense of purpose. These Americans will pat the violent vanguard of revolution on the head, content that they will not pay the price, all the while maintaining that those who crave law and order stand for regressive autocracy. Thus, Mayor Jenny Durkan of Seattle recently informed MSNBC that federal law enforcement attempting to stop destruction of federal property in Portland actually represented a "dry run for martial law."

With Democrats and those in the media willing to run cover for violent leftists, the thin veneer of civilization disintegrates. When violence is excused as speech and speech by the opposition labeled violence, democracies die. With each passing day of silence by those who should know better—or worse, those propagandizing on behalf of those who engage in criminal activity—America draws closer to the brink.

When the Counterculture Becomes the Culture

August 5, 2020

In November 2015, three years after taking the San Francisco 49ers to the Super Bowl, quarterback Colin Kaepernick was benched in favor of Blaine Gabbert, a career journeyman most recently unsuccessful with the Jacksonville Jaguars. The following preseason, Kaepernick began donning garb designed to mock police officers, including socks with cops dressed as pigs. He also remained seated for the national anthem during a preseason game, claiming, "I am not going to stand up to show pride in a flag for a country that oppresses black people and people of color."

At the time, multiple NFL players spoke out in opposition to Kaepernick's symbolic move: New York Giants wide receiver Victor Cruz said, "You've got to respect the flag, and you've got to stand up with your teammates. It's bigger than just you, in my opinion. You go up there; you're with a team; and you go and pledge your allegiance to the flag, and sing the national anthem with your team, and then you go about your business." At the time, this was a majority proposition: Seventy-two percent of Americans thought the gesture unpatriotic, according to a Reuters/Ipsos poll.

Kaepernick never regained a starting role in the NFL ... but his career took off again. He signed a lucrative endorsement deal with Nike to cash in on his supposed bravery; he cut a content deal with Disney. When he was offered a private tryout with NFL teams, he promptly violated all protocols and blew up the process. In June 2020, NFL commissioner Roger Goodell urged NFL teams to sign Kaepernick anyway. On July 4, Kaepernick tweeted: "Black ppl have been dehumanized, brutalized, criminalized + terrorized by America for centuries, & are expected to join your commemoration of 'independence,' while you enslaved our ancestors. We reject your celebration of white supremacy & look forward to liberation for all."

Today, Kaepernick's symbolism has become the new normal, morphed into a rote ritual of wokeness thanks to the ugly sight of then-Minneapolis police officer Derek Chauvin kneeling on the neck of George Floyd, who would later die. Democratic elected officials knelt in the halls of Congress. Major League Baseball players knelt before the national anthem to protest supposed systemic American racism. NBA players knelt as well, wearing Black Lives Matter T-shirts.

And players who refused to comply were publicly cudgeled. When San Francisco Giants pitcher Sam Coonrod refused to kneel, stating that he would not kneel for anything but God, he was castigated as benighted at best, racist at worst. When black Orlando Magic basketball player Jonathan Isaacs stood for the national anthem, again citing the unifying anti-racism of Christianity, he was ripped as "dangerous." Only Gregg Popovich, coach of the San Antonio Spurs, who has spent years utilizing purple progressive language about President Donald Trump, was exonerated for standing for the anthem—and that was because he wore a Black Lives Matter T-shirt.

So, what changed? Certainly not the data. Despite the presence of individual racism in American life in all walks of life, America's police are not systemically racist. Until the pandemic wrecked the economy across the board, black Americans were experiencing historic lows in unemployment and historic highs in median income. What changed is that Americans surrendered to the narrative promulgated for so long by those who seek to undermine American comity: that American history is not the story of moving toward the fulfillment of the promises of the Declaration of Independence but of the continuous, chameleonic perversion of bigotry; that America's founding ideas were lies, then and always; that only racial identity provides credence for talking about racial inequalities. The burden of proof has shifted to America's defenders.

And those defenders can never prove their case: first, because no country is perfect, and second, because systemic racism is a non-disprovable theory. Four short years ago, we mostly assumed the best of our fellow Americans—that they weren't endemically racist, at the very least—and the best of our country's ideals. No longer. The counterculture has become the culture. And that is both a tragedy and a travesty. There can be no future for a country in which standing for the national anthem is considered gauche, while kneeling is considered heroic.

Joe Biden's Awful Vice Presidential Pick

August 12, 2020

For well over a year, former Vice President Joe Biden has carried forth a simple strategy: Be nonthreatening. Facing a volatile, mistake-prone incumbent, Biden merely had to mimic vital signs, stay out of the spotlight and avoid looking off-putting or radical. And he accomplished those objectives, to great effect. He barely stumbled his way through the Democratic primaries, representing the nonradical voting repository for those alienated by the extremism of Sens. Bernie Sanders and Elizabeth Warren; he refused to kowtow to the Twitter blue checkmarks calling for him to endorse rioting and looting; he shied away from insane slogans about defunding the police. He stayed in the basement, playing prevent defense against President Donald Trump.

All he had before him was one final hurdle: picking a vice president.

Usually, the vice presidential pick means little or nothing. The vice presidency is a uniquely powerless office, and presidents rarely hand over power to their vice presidents. But Joe Biden will be 78 in November and appears to be slipping significantly mentally—despite CNN's protestations that he can still ride a bicycle. There is a reason nearly 6 in 10 Americans, according to a new Rasmussen poll, think Biden's vice president will finish his first term.

So Biden had one task: to pick a vice president who would appear nonthreatening, mainstream and generally normal. The onus would then lie with President Trump to shift the spotlight from his own campaign.

Biden couldn't do it.

He made an early error on that score when he declared publicly that he would pick a woman. This made it obvious that Biden was seeking a token—some sop for the woke progressives in his base. And that sop opened the door to further demands: the demand, for example, that he pick not merely a woman (or, as the woke left might have it, an individual with a cervix) but a black woman. And so Biden was trapped into a limited selection of politicians, ranging from the unknown (Rep. Val Demings of Florida) to the communist (Rep. Karen Bass of California), from the quietly sinister (former President Obama's national security advisor Susan Rice) to the loudly ridiculous (Georgia non-governor Stacey Abrams).

None of these picks would be great; some would be far worse than others. But there was one pick who would prove far worse than *all* the others: Sen. Kamala Harris, D-Calif. Harris is deeply radical. She endorsed "Medicare for All" while announcing that she would move Americans away from their private health care plans; she announced in open debate that she would use executive orders to ban "assault weapons"; she said she would ban fracking; she attacked Justice Brett Kavanaugh as a purported rapist and Judge Brian Buescher for his Catholicism. Harris is unpopular with many black Americans: As a prosecutor, she was fond of pursuing heavy sentences for light charges, as well as civil asset forfeiture—and then she bragged about smoking marijuana during her campaign. Harris has similarly alienated moderates, attacking Biden himself as a vicious racist for his unwillingness to support forced school busing in the 1970s, and suggesting that she believed Biden's sexual harassment accusers. There is a reason Harris utterly flamed out in the primaries, aside from her bizarre habit of breaking into a Joker-esque whoop when asked difficult questions.

Nothing about Harris screams nonthreatening. In fact, in her Machiavellian campaign manipulations, she appeared deeply threatening—threatening enough that Biden campaign adviser Chris Dodd reportedly wondered why Harris "had no remorse" for her opportunistic and dishonest attacks on Biden. At the very least, Biden should hire a food taster.

In selecting Harris, Biden has opened the door to the Trump campaign. And Trump should take full advantage. Biden's alleged moderation means nothing if he is willing to place Kamala Harris one heartbeat from the presidency. Biden's entire campaign strategy has now been undercut—all in a vain attempt to please the Twitterati, who will remain pleased for precisely seven seconds. Trump should be ecstatic. The race is on. And that's all on Biden.

The Remaking of the Middle East

August 18, 2020

This week, while all eyes have been on the Democratic National Convention taking place via Zoom, truly historic events have occurred in the Middle East: a long-awaited peace deal between Israel and the United Arab Emirates, including full normalization of relations; presumed peace deals to follow between Israel and Sudan, Oman and Bahrain; the possibility on the horizon of a similar deal with Saudi Arabia. These are not only historic events; they are unmitigated goods: the recognition of a Jewish state in the Middle East is the precondition to any peace in the Middle East. And the formation of a durable coalition to stave off the aggressive Islamism of Iran provides more stability and greater deterrence in the region.

It's easy to tell whether these are historic events by identifying those who oppose them. Iran is particularly angry; so is Iranian publicity agent Ben Rhodes, who served as former President Obama's deputy national security adviser. The tyrannical government of Turkey is deeply miffed; so is the terrorist government of the Palestinian Authority.

All are angry for the same reason: The central myth of American Middle Eastern policy, formulated over the course of decades, has been thoroughly exposed. That myth suggested that in order for any peace to bloom in the Middle East, the West would have to apply pressure on the Israeli government to make concessions to the Palestinians—that Israel would have to abandon claims to East Jerusalem, to the Golan Heights, to areas of Judea and Samaria.

That myth had been repeatedly tarnished by events of the last several years. When America moved her embassy to Jerusalem, foreign policy "experts" assured the public that the so-called Arab street would be set aflame. Instead, nothing happened. When America recognized Israel's formal annexation of the Golan Heights, foreign policy "experts" said that the Middle East would become a tinderbox. Nothing happened.

Now Arab nations are openly forming alliances with the Jewish state, fully acknowledging that Israeli-Palestinian issues remain bilateral in nature. Relations between Jordan and Israel; between the UAE and Israel; between Sudan and Israel; between Egypt and Israel—none now hide behind the fig leaf of Palestinian demands to avoid peace. They have realized that other interests, both economic and security-related, are a top priority. And they have tacitly recognized that Palestinian intransigence is not worthy of their support.

Hilariously, former Vice President Joe Biden tried to take credit for the Israel-UAE deal, suggesting that his own communications with the UAE had paved the way for the agreement. That's laughable on its face: In 2014, Biden had to issue a formal apology to the UAE government after suggesting that the UAE supported militants in Syria. Biden's chief contribution to the diplomatic breakthrough was actually the Obama administration's sycophantic embrace of the Iranian regime: By making clear that the United States could not be relied upon to protect Sunni nations from Iranian predations, the Obama administration convinced Arab nations that their interests lie in security alliance with Israel.

And so, the region has changed for the better. In more honest times, Trump administration officials who brokered this breakthrough would be up for the Nobel Peace Prize; instead, the news has been largely downplayed in favor of the scandal du jour from Trump's Twitter account. But we should be clear: The first important breakthrough in the Middle East in three decades just took place. And it took place because reality finally set in for Israel's heretofore enemies: Israel isn't going anywhere. Perhaps Palestinians will eventually learn the same lesson and peace will truly be possible.

Democrats Push Charges of Racism for Purposes of Convenience

August 26, 2020

In June 2019, Sen. Kamala Harris, D-Calif., tore into former Vice President Joe Biden in a Democratic primary debate. She openly suggested that he was a racist whose past political activity would have kept a "little girl" like her from attending integrated public school. About a year later, Biden selected Harris for his vice presidential candidate. It followed naturally that some intrepid reporter might ask Harris about why she had joined forces with such a historic bigot.

So far, Harris has been asked that question twice. Stephen Colbert asked, obviously assuming that she had prepared an answer. She hadn't. Instead, Harris broke into her now-famous Awkward Joker Cackle, saying with a laugh, "It was a debate!" Colbert quickly tried to laugh with her to alleviate the extraordinary tension—and to back away from the unforced revelation that Harris is simply a political hack willing to leverage charges of racism for career gain.

Now, political observers might figure that such a terrifying brush with unmasking might prompt Harris to think through the question. She still hasn't. Over the weekend, ABC News' Robin Roberts asked Harris the same question. And Harris' answer was no better: "I think that that conversation is a distraction from what we need to accomplish right now and what we need to do." Harris again confirmed that her allegations of racism against Biden were merely a tool in her arsenal—a tool to be wielded when convenient and stored away for possible future use when not.

Unfortunately, Harris isn't the only political figure who sees charges of racism as a convenient weapon, rather than as serious allegations requiring actual evidence. Democratic politicians appear to have latched on to the simple joys of charging political opponents with racism at the drop of a hat. According to the Associated Press, Democrats have taken, for example, to charging those who mispronounce Harris' first name with racism—as though it is perfectly obvious that the emphasis in "Kamala" lies on the first syllable rather than the second.

And it's not merely that Democrats now levy frivolous racism charges with ease. Democrats are willing to jump—without any evidence and to dire consequence—to the conclusion that any incident involving black Americans is rife with racism. Thus, this week, when a black man named Jacob Blake in Kenosha, Wisconsin, was shot by police officers and video leading up to the shooting was released, Democrats rushed to condemn the police, even while *explicitly acknowledging that they didn't have the facts.*

Biden released a statement with staggering irresponsibility: He called for an "immediate, full and transparent investigation" but openly stated that "the officers must be held accountable"; he claimed that America had woken up "yet again with grief and outrage that yet another black American is a victim of excessive force"; he called the shooting an "inflection point" and yet another symptom of "systemic racism." Again, Biden had no access to the facts. But that didn't stop him from levying charges of racism.

It wasn't just Biden. Gov. Tony Evers, D-Wis.—whose state investigative system will be handling the case—immediately announced, "While we do not have all of the details yet, what we know for certain is that he is not the first Black man or person to have been shot or injured or mercilessly killed at the hands of individuals in law enforcement in our state or our country."

And so, Kenosha burned. And the narrative has been set: The shooting was unjustified, and racist at that. No evidence has been presented; none need be. And if the facts don't match the accusations, the facts will be put aside. Harris herself has continued to push the absolute lie, for example, that Michael Brown was murdered in Ferguson, Missouri, an allegation firmly rebutted by former President Obama's Department of Justice. Fealty to the narrative is the sole qualifier for power in Democratic circles.

Will any of this alleviate racism? Of course not. But it's not designed to. It's designed to achieve and attain power. And, so far, the strategy seems to be working.

Why Won't Biden Condemn Antifa or BLM Violence?

September 2, 2020

On Monday, Democratic presidential nominee Joe Biden was finally forced to confront the left-wing violence that has been plaguing America's major cities for months on end: riots in New York, Washington, D.C., Los Angeles, Chicago, Portland and Seattle, among other cities. For a full week, the Democratic National Convention ignored that ongoing violence, driven by members of the Black Lives Matter and antifa movements. The media went right along with the narrative that violent riots have been "mostly peaceful," that conservatives were "pouncing" on occasional violence for political purposes and that the true threat to American safety could be found in Donald Trump's Twitter feed.

The only solution to America's ills, Biden held, could be found in repeating pernicious slogans about supposed systemic American racism. On Aug. 9, Biden tweeted: "It's been six years since Michael Brown's life was taken in Ferguson—reigniting a movement. We must continue the work of tackling systemic racism and reforming policing." Never mind that two state investigations and the Obama Department of Justice found that Brown was justifiably shot; no facts are necessary to continue repeating mantras.

Then, a small Wisconsin town, Kenosha, burst into flames.

At first, the media tried to excuse the burning, rioting and looting. After all, they proclaimed, this was justified rage at the systemic racism of American policing. It simply didn't matter that Jacob Blake, who was shot by police, had resisted arrest, bucked police officers off of him, ignored their orders and then reached into his vehicle, where a knife was later found on the driver's side floorboards. It also didn't matter that Blake has faced vicious criminal charges and had an open warrant for sexual assault and domestic violence—and that the police reportedly arrived only after being called by a woman who alleged that Blake digitally raped her in front of one of her children. The police were the problem.

And Biden went right along with that generalized narrative, excoriating the police for the shooting of Jacob Blake. Sure, Biden may have softly tut-tutted violence. But the *real* problem was the American system. On Aug. 28, Biden tweeted that George Floyd and Blake can't become "just another pair of hashtags," and that instead, it was time to "reverse systemic racism."

But Americans didn't see the riots and looting in Kenosha as indicative of a reaction to American racism. They saw it for what it was: horrific behavior. And so, Biden was forced to leave his basement—to fly to Pennsylvania, of all places, and deliver a 12-minute address denouncing violence.

The media did their dutiful best to characterize that address as a groundbreaking call for peace. It was no such thing. Instead, Biden blamed the police, Trump and white supremacists for the violence. He name-checked "right-wing militias" and "white supremacists." He made no mention of Black Lives Matter or antifa, the actual sources of rioting and looting in American cities. And the same media that excoriated Trump for condemning violence "on many sides" in Charlottesville suddenly found it in their hearts to pretend that Biden's radically unspecific rhetoric actually covered the evils of BLM and antifa.

Biden simply cannot condemn antifa or BLM by name, because to do so would be to recognize two simple truths: first, that Trump isn't the chief source of violence in American cities; second, that in spite of his "return to normalcy" message, Biden's "systemic racism" narrative provides the ideological groundwork for those who seek to tear down the system. Democrats have spent months denying the violence, calling Trump a fascist for offering federal help and decrying the American system. The fruits are on full display for everyone to see. And so, Biden must bluff, and the media must cover for him.

Perhaps Biden will get away with it. Americans should hope he doesn't.

The Democrats Pick the Criminal

September 9, 2020

On Aug. 23, 29-year-old Jacob Blake, a black man, was shot seven times in the back by a white police officer. The original video, which only included the last moments of the incident, gave no context for the incident. But further video and police reports made clear what happened.

According to the police association, the police were called to the scene by a black woman who had dialed 911 to report that Blake was attempting to steal the keys to her car. There was an open warrant on Blake for third-degree felony sexual assault; the alleged victim is the woman who dialed 911, and she apparently had a restraining order against Blake. Back in May, she alleged that Blake entered a room where she was sleeping near one of her children, thrust his finger into her vagina, pulled it out, smelled it and said, "Smells like you've been with other men." The alleged victim also said that Blake sexually assaults her approximately twice per year.

Upon arriving at the scene, the police attempted to effectuate an arrest. Blake resisted. He apparently got one of the officers in a headlock and resisted two separate uses of a stun gun. He then disobeyed officer commands, walked around to the driver's side of an SUV and reached inside. A knife was found on the driver's side floorboards.

This is the definition of a justified shoot, by all available evidence. Yet Democratic presidential candidate Joe Biden and vice presidential candidate Kamala Harris have chosen to side with an alleged rapist and against police officers attempting to do their job.

On Sept. 2, Biden said he thought that the officers in Blake's shootings should be charged, adding, "Let's make sure justice is done." Harris—whose judgment on these matters ought to be doubted, given her conviction that Michael Brown was murdered and Supreme Court Justice Brett Kavanaugh was a probable rapist—agreed that the officer "should be charged."

But Biden and Harris didn't stop there. Biden traveled to Kenosha and met with Blake's family. Biden got on the phone with Blake—who was handcuffed to his hospital bed, since he is currently under arrest—and quoted the book of Psalms, adding that "nothing is going to defeat" Blake. Harris went further, telling Blake she was "proud" of him and saying that the Blake family is "incredible"—an amazing description of a family wherein the son is an alleged rapist and the father is an open anti-Semite, according to his public social media posts.

The New York Times provided cover for this insulting insanity in a long puff piece about Blake, describing him as a hero who "survived and has begun to tell his own story." That piece left any description of his crimes to paragraph 17 and never mentioned that he resisted arrest and had a knife in the vehicle.

On a raw level, none of this makes sense. Blake is, by all available evidence, a villain. The police officer was, by all available evidence, acting within the scope of his duty. But in the context of a broader Democratic narrative that police are systemically racist, and that all criminals of minority ethnicity are victims of that system, it all makes perfect sense. If you think that American racism is responsible for a black man allegedly raping a black woman, this is a story in which there are only victims and there is no perpetrator but the system itself—in this case, a system represented by the white police officer.

If we wish to live together in a society, this perspective cannot win. By lionizing Jacob Blake while decrying the police who tried to arrest him, Democrats justify and incentivize criminality. This must stop. Individuals are responsible for their crimes; police are necessary to stop those crimes. Those who disagree cannot be allowed to gain power.

Lawn-Sign Virtue Signaling and the Death of Politics

September 16, 2020

This week, America's West Coast found itself on fire. Millions of acres have burned across California, Oregon and Washington. The smoke clouds have been so immense that they have blotted out the sun in certain areas; air quality has been so poor that hundreds of thousands of people have been forced indoors.

There are several key reasons for the extent of these wildfires. Federal and state policies have been geared around stifling wildfires for decades, rather than allowing controlled burns to prevent accretion of flammable vegetation. As ProPublica reports, California alone saw the burning of 4.4 million to 11 million acres per year prehistorically; between 1999 and 2017, that number dropped to only 13,000 acres per year; in February 2020, Nature Sustainability concluded that California would need to burn some 20 million acres to restabilize in terms of fire. Meanwhile, even those who pursue controlled burns must jump through extraordinarily regulatory hoops to do so: The Clean Air Act treats smoke from controlled burns as a pollutant, for example.

Even California Gov. Gavin Newsom admitted to President Donald Trump that the state had botched its fire policy: "We have not done justice for our forest management." But that admission was the mere precursor to a more important point for Newsom: that climate change is truly to blame for the wildfires. "The science is in ... that climate change is real," Newsom lectured Trump.

In reality, climate change may have had some effect on the California wildfires, but that effect is entirely secondary in scope to the effect of bad policy. According to the Environmental Protection Agency, the temperature in Southern California has increased approximately 3 degrees F over the past century. Since 1980, the temperature in California has increased less than 2 degrees F. Does climate change exacerbate dryness and heat? Of course. But fire policy was the chief failure here.

What's more, no matter what Trump believes on climate change, the science is clear: Nothing Trump could have done would have made a measurable impact on the climate between 2017 and 2020. In fact, if the entire United States were to cease carbon emissions today, the climate would be just 0.17 degrees C less hot by 2100.

Yet the media and Democrats suggested that the true story of the wildfires was indeed climate change. This theme was trumpeted by Democratic presidential candidate Joe Biden first and foremost: Biden emerged from his basement long enough to stand before a field of waving grass and explain that Trump's unwillingness to signal proper concern about climate change would kill Americans. "We have four more years of Trump's climate denial," Biden gravely intoned. "How many suburbs will be burned in wildfires?"

The answer: exactly as many as would be burned with four years of Biden governance. But the point here isn't shaping public policy; it's shaping perception. Politics has become about the art of the lawn sign.

In California, there's one lawn sign that has become quite popular. It reads, "IN THIS HOUSE, WE BELIEVE: BLACK LIVES MATTER; WOMEN'S RIGHTS ARE HUMAN RIGHTS; NO HUMAN IS ILLEGAL; SCIENCE IS REAL; LOVE IS LOVE; KINDNESS IS EVERYTHING." The sign is generally plunked in the front yard of a nice suburban home, where it acts as a sort of unearned symbol of virtue. The semantically overloaded tautologies are designed to act as a dissociation tactic from supposedly benighted fellow Americans who apparently *don't* believe "SCIENCE IS REAL" or that "KINDNESS IS EVERYTHING."

But, of course, the sign conveys nothing beyond a self-congratulatory insistence that the sign owner is a better human than other humans. By phrases like "SCIENCE IS REAL," the sign owner conveys that if you attribute California wildfires to anything beyond

Trumpian evil and climate change, you deny science. Which is anti-scientific, of course.

But it's effective. That's why New York Gov. Andrew Cuomo tweeted, "Science knows" (cynics might point out that science suggests shipping COVID-19-positive seniors into nursing homes is idiotic). That's why Dr. Jill Biden tweeted, "#VoteForScience" (cynics might ask whether she believes a woman can become a man). By portraying your lack of a political program as entirely irrelevant to the *broader* question of Science Denial, you can avoid the hard conversations politics was intended to address.

Lawn signs don't solve problems. But they do make us feel good. Which is what politics are supposed to achieve nowadays in the absence of actual solutions. Perhaps at some point we might ask why politics make us feel so rotten these days.

Democrats Threaten to Burn Down the Republic to Stack the Supreme Court

September 24, 2020

Last week, Supreme Court Justice Ruth Bader Ginsburg died at the age of 87. Her death immediately initiated a political firestorm in Washington, D.C.—one that threatens the very integrity of the republic. That's not because, as the media and Democrats would claim, some sort of institutional norm has been violated by a Republican president selecting a replacement for Ginsburg to be voted on by a Republican Senate. It's because Democrats have declared that so long as they are unable to replace Ginsburg with an activist left-wing judge willing to use the Constitution to cram down liberal policy prescriptions, they will tear down every barrier to majoritarian tyranny.

The Constitution was specifically constructed to promote gridlock. That's because the Founding Fathers greatly feared majoritarian tyranny—legalized mob rule by which simple majorities could cram down violations of rights on minorities. To that end, they balanced the House of Representatives, which was popularly elected, and the Senate, which was represented by state and selected by state legislatures. They balanced the legislative branch with the executive and judicial branches. They balanced power between a federal structure and state governments. The founders believed that the greatest protection for individual rights lay in ambition checking ambition at every level.

Progressives have, since the beginning of the 20th century, objected to this philosophy of government. Instead, they have seen institutional gridlock as a danger to "getting things done." Former

President Woodrow Wilson infamously explained that "Men as communities are supreme over men as individuals," and that, therefore, there ought to be no institutional checks against governmental necessity. Democrats have faithfully carried forward that vision, checked only by political reality—Wilson unconstitutionally expanded the executive branch; Franklin Roosevelt infamously sought to pack the Supreme Court; Lyndon Johnson radically expanded the size and scope of the federal government; Barack Obama declared that the government itself "is us."

That meant that for the political left, all institutions of government had to be converted into instruments of power or destroyed. The left has done just that with the Supreme Court for generations, viewing it as a repository for transformational change rather than a legal body with a mandate to only interpret honestly the words of the law. With that view of the court threatened by a Republican-appointed majority, Democrats are now panicking.

And they are responding with radical threats to break *every* check and balance. This week, Democrats openly threatened to destroy the Senate filibuster, a traditional mechanism for restraining bare majorities, most recently used by Democrats themselves to stymie COVID-19 relief funding. They also threatened to add new states to the union, specifically citing federal territories they believe will elect Democrats; and to pack the Supreme Court, reestablishing a Democratic-appointed majority by adding new seats.

These actions aren't merely violative of constitutional principles and the founding philosophy. They are dangerous. Imagine a 55-vote Democratic majority in a 104-seat body, cramming through a gun confiscation measure, greenlit by a 13-member court packed by Democrats. Will red states simply acquiesce to this overt seizure of power, to this absurd rewriting of the constitutional bargain? Why should they?

All of which means that the 2020 presidential race has now become a referendum on the Democrats, not President Donald Trump. Democratic candidate Joe Biden's inherent campaign pledge was a return to stability, not a leap into revolution. But by threatening the institutional architecture, Biden's campaign has become just that. Now Americans will be forced to choose between the vulgarity of Donald Trump—a vulgarity and boorishness, however off-putting, that has not threatened constitutional rights—and a vengeful Democratic Party threatening to remold the country from the top down.

Why I'm Leaving California

September 3, 2020

My family and my company are leaving California.

It's heartbreaking.

My parents moved to California four decades ago. I grew up here. For 33 of the 36 years I've spent on this planet, I've lived here. I was born at St. Joseph's in Burbank; I attended elementary school at Edison Elementary; I went to college at UCLA. I co-founded a major media company here, with 75 employees in Los Angeles. I met my wife here; all three of my kids are native Californians.

This is the most beautiful state in the country. The climate is incredible. The scenery is amazing. The people are generally warm, and there's an enormous amount to do.

And we're leaving.

We're leaving because all the benefits of California have steadily eroded—and then suddenly collapsed. Meanwhile, all the costs of California have steadily increased—and then suddenly skyrocketed. It can be difficult to spot the incremental encroachment of a terrible disease, but once the final ravages set in, it becomes obvious that the illness is fatal. So, too, with California, where bad governance has turned a would-be paradise into a burgeoning dystopia.

When my family moved to North Hollywood, I was 11. We lived in a safe, clean suburb. Yes, Los Angeles had serious crime and homelessness problems, but those were problems relegated to pockets of the city—problems that, with good governance, we thought could eventually be healed. Instead, the government allowed those problems to metastasize. As of 2011, Los Angeles County counted less than 40,000 homeless; as of 2020, that number had skyrocketed to 66,000. Suburban areas have become the sites of homeless encampments.

Nearly every city underpass hosts a tent city; the city, in its kindness, has put out port-a-potties to reduce the possibility of COVID-19 spread.

Police are forbidden in most cases from either moving transients or even moving their garbage. Nearly every public space in Los Angeles has become a repository for open waste, needles and trash. The most beautiful areas of Los Angeles, from Santa Monica beach to my suburb, have become wrecks. My children have personally witnessed drug use, public urination and public nudity. Looters were allowed free reign in the middle of the city during the Black Lives Matter riots; Rodeo Drive was closed at 1 p.m., and citizens were curfewed at 6 p.m.

To combat these trends, local and state governments have gamed the statistics, reclassifying offenses and letting prisoners go free. Meanwhile, the police have become targets for public ire. In July, the city of Los Angeles slashed police funding, cutting the force to its lowest levels in over a decade.

At the same time, taxes have risen. California's top marginal income tax rate is now 13.3%; legislators want to raise it to 16.8%. California is also home to a 7.25% sales tax, a 50-cent gas tax and a bevy of other taxes that drain the wallet and burden business. California has the worst regulatory climate in America, according to CEO Magazine's survey of 650 CEOs. The public-sector unions essentially make public policy, running up the debt while providing fewer and fewer actual services. California's public education system is a massive failure, and even its once-great colleges are now burdened by the stupidities of political correctness, including an unwillingness to use standardized testing.

And still, the state legislature is dominated by Democrats. California is not on a trajectory toward recovery; it is on a trajectory toward oblivion. Taxpayers are moving out—now including my family and my company. In 2019, before the pandemic and the widespread rioting and looting, outmigration jumped 38%, rising for the seventh straight year. That number will increase again this year.

I want my kids to grow up safe. I want them to grow up in a community with a future, with more freedom and safety than I grew up with. California makes that impossible. So, goodbye, Golden State. Thanks for the memories.

If Trump Loses, It's on Trump

October 7, 2020

Joe Biden is a terrible candidate.

He is 77 years old; he is incoherent; he has called a "lid" every other day of his campaign to avoid serious questioning. His running mate, Sen. Kamala Harris, is so unpopular that she dropped out of the Democratic primaries before they even reached her home state. The Biden-Harris campaign is absolutely lackluster.

And according to national polling, Joe Biden is leading incumbent President Donald Trump by up to 16 points. In the RealClearPolitics polling average, Trump is trailing Biden in every single swing state. Were the election held today, by the RealClearPolitics statistics, Biden would win 375 electoral votes, picking up states including North Carolina, Georgia, Virginia, Arizona, Michigan, Wisconsin and Pennsylvania.

How is this happening? How did a doddering fool, a career politician mostly famous for his incurable logorrhea, end up in the catbird seat one month before the 2020 election?

The answer is simple: Joe Biden understands the nature of this election. Donald Trump simply does not.

To understand this election does not require a graduate course in political science: If the election is a referendum on President Trump, he will lose; if the election is a referendum on Joe Biden, he will lose. Trump is personally unpopular by every poll metric, and he has been consistently unpopular for years, but he was still able to win in 2016 because Hillary Clinton was even less popular. The same could have held true here.

After all, Biden has opened himself wide to serious questioning. He has repeatedly refused to state whether he is in favor of ending the

Senate filibuster, adding new states and packing the Supreme Court, calling such questions distractions; he has refused to condemn the antifa movement; he has soft-pedaled Black Lives Matter violence in America's major cities; he has put forward the most left-wing platform in American history, according to communist fellow traveler Bernie Sanders.

But Biden hasn't answered a single serious question. He has been able to avoid nearly all questions by pointing at his opponent. Biden hasn't just run a lackluster campaign; he hasn't run *any* campaign. He hasn't even walked a campaign. He has essentially grown into his couch in his Delaware basement, getting out only long enough to stand in front of an empty field or answer a few softball questions from a friendly pseudo-journalist.

That's not just because the media hate Trump and sycophantically massage Biden, though they do. It's because Trump himself steadfastly refuses to recognize the central issue of the campaign: his own centrality. Trump *loves* being the center of attention, and he simply refuses to cede the spotlight. Every day is a new spectacle in Trumpland, from descending in Marine One onto the White House lawn amid dramatic music to reenter quarantine to tweeting incessantly about the latest news of the day. The media hang on Trump's every word, and he appears to love that.

But that symbiotic relationship between Trump and the media puts Trump at a dramatic disadvantage. The more people think about Trump, the less they want to. In 2016, the "Access Hollywood" tape unintentionally relegated Trump to the sidelines in the last days of the campaign, freeing the way for then-FBI Director James Comey to put the spotlight squarely on Hillary Clinton's emails—and Trump won. In 2018, Democrats seized the spotlight by unjustly and cruelly maligning Justice Brett Kavanaugh, and the polls consequently tightened; then Trump seized the spotlight back by talking about illegal immigrant caravans, and Democrats won.

Joe Biden has learned the lesson. Biden has spent this campaign pointing at Trump. Trump, who should be pointing at Biden, is too busy pointing at himself. Unless Trump somehow suppresses his ego enough to allow Biden to become the issue, Trump is likely to exit the political stage altogether come Nov. 3.

Why Democrats Hate Amy Coney Barrett

October 14, 2020

This week, Democrats struggled to explain why Judge Amy Coney Barrett should not be confirmed to serve on the Supreme Court. They trotted out hackneyed arguments, suggesting that some political norm had been broken by a Republican president nominating a judge to be confirmed as a justice by a Republican Senate in an election year. There have been 19 times where a seat became vacant in an election year and both the presidency and Senate were controlled by the same party, resulting in 17 judicial confirmations. They suggested that Ruth Bader Ginsburg's dying wish to leave her seat open until a Democrat takes power represented a sort of binding legal commitment.

And they fumed.

They fumed that Barrett refuses to pledge fealty to their political priorities. They fumed that Barrett has stated that the role of the judiciary is *not* to achieve moral ends but to enforce the law. They fumed that Barrett had the temerity to state that "courts are not designed to solve every problem or right every wrong in our public life," that "the policy decisions and value judgments of government must be made by the political branches" and that she has done her utmost to "reach the result required by the law," whatever her preferences might be.

That's because, in the view of the political left, the court ought to be merely another weapon in its political arsenal. Conservatives see the judiciary as Alexander Hamilton characterized it in "Federalist No. 78": as the "least dangerous" branch, capable of "neither force nor will, but merely judgment," an institution whose legitimacy rests on its unwillingness to "exercise WILL instead of JUDGMENT." Liberals see the court as a super-legislature, designed to act as moral arbiters on behalf of progressive values. That's why former President Barack Obama stated that judges ought to be selected for the quality of "empathy, of understanding and identifying with people's hopes and struggles, as an essential ingredient for arriving at just decisions and outcomes."

Critical legal theorists have suggested that conservatives are fibbing—that their view of the judiciary as relegated to judgment alone is merely cover for the reinforcement of their political priorities. But the data suggest otherwise. During the 2019 Supreme Court term, for example, out of some 67 decisions, the four justices appointed by Democrats voted together 51 times; Republican appointees only voted together 37 times. As Ilya Shapiro of the Cato Institute has pointed out, "it's the (Ruth Bader) Ginsburg Four that represent a bloc geared toward progressive policy outcomes." Republican appointees, in other words, are politically heterodox significantly more often than Democratic appointees. That's because, on a fundamental level, they take their job—and the constitutional separation of powers—seriously.

Democrats do not. That's why they see as the glories of the Supreme Court those moments in which the Supreme Court seized power on behalf of progressive ideals. Roe v. Wade has become holy writ on the political left, specifically because it robbed the American people of their right to vote on the issue of abortion. Democrats see nothing but glory in Supreme Court justices seizing authority to protect abortion on behalf of defining "one's own concept of existence, of meaning, of the universe, and of the mystery of human life" (Planned Parenthood v. Casey, 1992). They see nothing but wonder in Supreme Court justices declaring that the judiciary has been delegated enforcement of "a charter protecting the right of all persons to enjoy liberty as we learn its meaning" (Obergefell v. Hodges, 2015). They see nothing but cause for celebration in the Supreme Court cramming down on the American people their own sense of our "evolving standards of decency" (Trop v. Dulles, 1958) or the importance of never-before-defined "emanations" and "penumbras" (Griswold v. Connecticut, 1965). They want the court to act as an oligarchy.

And they are angry that Barrett's nomination has moved the court away from that progressive, oligarchic rule. That's why they're threatening to pack the court—because they wish to restore that oligarchy to power. And that's just another reason why, for all the talk about Donald Trump's threats to core American institutions, he can't hold a candle to even mainstream Democratic willingness to trash checks and balances on behalf of power.

The Media Officially Becomes the Communications Department for Joe Biden

October 21, 2020

This week, the New York Post published a bombshell story. Hunter Biden's laptop was apparently given to a computer repairman in Delaware, and a copy of the hard drive was turned over to the Post. The Post found several alarming emails. The first was a communique from a Ukrainian businessman from the natural gas company Burisma—the same company from which Hunter Biden would gain a reported $50,000-per-month salary as a board member, despite knowing nothing about Ukraine or natural gas. The communique contained the businessman's thanks to Hunter for brokering a meeting with Joe Biden.

This was mildly damning, considering that Joe had blithely informed the world that he knew nothing of his ne'er-do-well son's foreign activities. What was more damning was an email thread that appeared to concern proposed compensation packages from the now-defunct CEFC China Energy Co. That thread identified Hunter as "Chair/Vice Chair depending on agreement with CEFC," with a proposed equity split of "20" for "H" (presumably Hunter) and "10 held by H for the big guy." A Fox News source privy to the thread confirmed that the "big guy" was Joe Biden. An apparent text from Hunter to one of his children contained this tantalizing suggestion: "(U)nlike Pop, I won't make you give me half your salary."

All of this would, in a normal world, prompt the media to ask Biden about the emails. Instead, the media have halfheartedly questioned Biden, who has promptly dismissed all questions, calling them a "smear campaign" and even suggesting that a CBS reporter was biased against him. The New York Times' Maggie Haberman was ripped up and down for even tweeting a link to the Post story; Politico's Jake Sherman abjectly apologized for having tweeted the story.

Other media members have overtly made the case that the story shouldn't be taken seriously. NBC News' Andrea Mitchell reported that the email scandal could be Russian disinformation; Politico reported that 50 former intelligence officials posited that the story was indeed Russian disinformation. In this, they followed the lead of Democratic Rep. Adam Schiff, who claimed, without evidence, that the Biden story was a Russian dirty trick—despite the fact that director of national intelligence John Ratcliffe openly denied such speculation.

Meanwhile, Biden has deployed his campaign surrogates to television to insist that the reports are "unconfirmed." Not one surrogate denied that the emails were authentic or bothered to explain them.

But Biden hasn't had to explain. His protectors aren't relegated to the media. They also encompass the Big Tech heads, who quickly cracked down on dissemination of the Post story itself. Twitter banned tweeting of the link and suspended accounts that tried to spread it, including that of White House press secretary Kayleigh McEnany. Facebook announced that even though the story hadn't been fact-checked or found to be false, the company would suppress its reach in anticipation of such fact-checking.

There is no doubt that Big Tech's decision was political—or that the media's hesitancy to cover the Biden allegations is similarly political. Both Big Tech and the media, staffed thoroughly with Democrats, are gun-shy about the prospect of turning the election toward President Donald Trump. If they err, they would far rather err on the side of Joe Biden than the side of journalistic aggressiveness. The last thing they want is getting the blame if Biden somehow blows the White House.

This is all deeply dangerous. At a time when our trust in media is already low, the media have thoroughly debunked themselves as neutral arbiters of fact. At a time when social media has consolidated unprecedented power to control the information seen by Americans, social media overseers have decided to bottleneck information they don't like. Americans rightly distrust the journalistic establishment. They are right, too, to question whether they are being allowed to read stories that cut against the priorities of Silicon Valley Leftists.

The result of journalistic and social media overreach will not be Americans' quiet acquiescence to the new Informational Elite. It will be frustration and anger.

The Great COVID Lie

October 28, 2020

Until COVID-19 hit, President Donald Trump was on a glide path to reelection. On domestic policy, Trump's tax and regulatory cuts spurred the economy to heights unseen in 50 years; his Department of Education cracked down on the star-chamber courts applied on college campuses in cases of alleged sexual misconduct; he has appointed scores of well-qualified constitutionalist judges, including three Supreme Court justices. On foreign policy, Trump is the first president of my lifetime not to enter any foreign wars; he has brokered historic peace deals in the Middle East between Israel and Arab countries; he has stood up to Chinese predations in unprecedented ways.

If this election had been held in February, Trump likely would have won. And he likely would have won rather easily. That's because Trump's often-terrible rhetoric would have taken a back seat to his actions, and Americans' pessimism about Trump's character would have taken a back seat to their optimism about his agenda.

Then COVID hit.

The economy, thanks in large part to overwrought lockdown policies, collapsed. Hundreds of thousands of Americans died. And Trump's rhetoric blunders took on renewed seriousness as Americans looked for steady leadership and instead found the usual Trumpian stew of bloviation and exaggeration and ire.

COVID has become the Democrats' chief electioneering ploy. Their argument is patently wrong and immoral. It is an argument repeated ad nauseum by Joe Biden and Kamala Harris, as well as their allies in the media. The argument, expressed by Biden, is this: "220,000 Americans dead ... Anyone who's responsible for that many deaths should not remain as president of the United States of America."

But, of course, Trump isn't responsible for those deaths. Trump should have spoken sooner about wearing masks; he should have acted with more alacrity in developing testing. But COVID has spread throughout the world, killing hundreds of thousands, and is now spreading nearly unchecked throughout Europe, where lockdowns and masking have been prevalent for months. In fact, Democratic governors praised Trump for giving them the ventilators and personal protective equipment they sought; the White House's Operation Warp Speed has accelerated the development of a vaccine in historically unprecedented ways. The hardest-hit states in terms of death per millions were nearly all states with governors who did *not* follow Trump's preferred anti-lockdown policies.

Just as important, Democrats have never provided an alternative plan with regard to COVID. Biden's stated plan—to accelerate a vaccine, to socially distance, to mask more, to create local authority for targeted lockdowns—is no different from Trump's. Biden was holding packed rallies into early March. Democrats have repeatedly condoned or celebrated massive rallies of millions of people during the pandemic, so long as those rallies meet with their political approval.

The narrative that Trump is responsible for COVID'S death toll, then, is a religious argument, not a factual one. It is reliant on a perverse view of the universe by which Trump is responsible for all evil, a miasmatic orange Satan haunting the land. And, the theory goes, if Trump is excised, COVID will be controlled by someone with a steadier hand.

That's nonsense. The pandemic will continue on Nov. 4, no matter who is elected. But so long as Trump is labeled the true scourge, rather than COVID, Trump will pay the political price. And the so-called Party of Science will continue to promote that anti-scientific lie all the way up through Election Day.

The Woke Lose

November 4, 2020

On Tuesday night, the American people spoke. They spoke with millions upon millions of voices to produce the greatest presidential election voter turnout in over a century. And they sent a variety of messages, most of them quite positive.

Voters rejected the prevailing narratives of a media determined to make the election a pure referendum on Donald Trump's character. Even if Joe Biden prevails eventually, he will likely be faced with a Republican Senate majority and a 2022 contest that will put the House of Representatives squarely in Republican sights.

Voters rejected the pollsters' overconfident modeling: Pollsters were dramatically wrong in their national numbers and just as wrong in their Senate estimates. Voters apparently aren't all that interested in registering their opinions with elite firms who see them as social science subjects rather than as individuals.

Voters stuck to their guns in red states; they stuck to their guns in blue states; they stuck to their guns in purple states. America is divided, and it is not growing less divided just out of the elitists' overwrought and hysterical mewling about Trump. This is still a country that is one-third conservative, one-third liberal and one-third in the middle.

But one message resonated above all others: the outright rejection of the ongoing quest by Democrats and the media to paint Americans into racial categories and then declare demographics destiny. Donald Trump bucked four long years of Democrats and media members labeling both him and his supporters white supremacists, bigots and homophobes. He refused to be cowed by a media determined to paint him as a racist for refusing the faulty premise that America is institutionally bigoted. And he won an increased share of black and Hispanic voters.

According to Edison exit polling, as of election night, Trump had gained 2 points with white women; 4 points with black men and 4 points with black women; 3 points with Latino men and 3 points with Latino women; and 5 points in the "other" category. In Florida, according to NBC News exit polling, Trump's coalition included a 55% share of the Cuban American vote, a 30% share of the Puerto Rican vote and 48% of "other Latinos." Trump substantially elevated the national share of Latino and black voters for Republicans—and did so without pandering on illegal immigration or buying into the trite and ugly lies of the Black Lives Matter movement.

It wasn't just Trump. In California, a majority-minority state, voters refused to greenlight the racist Proposition 16, which would have repealed a state constitutional provision banning racial discrimination, paving the way for reparations and affirmative action. They did so by a margin of over 10 points and despite the fact that Prop 16 advocates spent 12 times the money their opponents did.

All of this has sent woke thinkers into spasms of apoplexy. The execrable Nikole Hannah-Jones, creator of the pseudo-historical "1619 Project," tweeted out that Latinos can no longer be considered a racial category, since some Cubans are "white." Charles Blow of The New York Times tweeted, "We are surrounded by racists."

Actually, Hannah-Jones and Blow aren't surrounded by racists. They're surrounded by people who reject racism and reject the implicitly racist belief that ethnicity ought to dictate voting pattern.

All of this is excellent news. Americans spoke last night. They spoke *as Americans*, as individuals, not as members of contrived interest groups. And that is certainly worth celebrating.

When 'Unity' Means 'Shut the Hell Up'

November 11, 2020

On Saturday evening, presidential frontrunner Joe Biden—who doesn't actually become president-elect until vote counts are certified—gave a preliminary victory address. In that address, he spoke of his mandate to govern: a mandate, he said, that extended to marshalling the "forces of decency ... fairness ... science ... hope." Which is a pretty vague mandate, as it turns out.

But there was another overarching mandate Biden expressed: a mandate to come together, to unify as Americans. "To make progress, we must stop treating our opponents as our enemy," Biden said. "We are not enemies. We are Americans."

All of that is nice. Who wouldn't like a country in which we could enjoy cultural events together without being lectured about the alleged evils of the country, in which we could attend family events without being castigated as bigots, in which we could disagree and still enjoy one another? Who wouldn't like an America in which our neighbors no longer see us as cancel-culture targets, in which we no longer have to fear our compatriots rioting and looting over supposed systemic injustices, in which our social interactions are not limited by our voter registration?

But.

Americans are right to have some rather serious trust issues with calls for unity in our polarized time. After all, former President Barack Obama pledged American reunification right up until he began treating tea partyers as unspeakable threats and political opponents as crypto-racists. Everything was hopey and changey right up until the time ... it wasn't.

So, in order to earn our trust, Joe Biden would have to call *his own side* out for raising the temperature. And he has steadfastly refused to do so. He hasn't called out Black Lives Matter for the suggestion that America is systemically racist; he has cheered it on. He hasn't condemned antifa; he has deemed it a philosophy rather than a dangerous movement. And he certainly hasn't said a word about the continuing attacks on Trump supporters.

We will wait in vain for Biden to chide former first lady Michelle Obama for declaring that 70 million Americans "voted for the status quo, even when it meant supporting lies, hate, chaos, and division." Our bones will likely bleach before Biden tells Hillary Clinton that Trump supporters aren't deplorables.

No, "unity" in the Biden formulation isn't a recognition of what we have in common; it's a demand that we silence ourselves in order to mirror Biden's priorities. Unity, you see, can be achieved one of two ways: through recognition of the other, through a determination to understand those who think differently than we do; or through ideological domination. It's rather obvious which pathway Democrats will choose. After all, social ostracization is one of their most powerful tools. Why disarm now?

Americans can only come together when we share a common philosophy, history and culture. Democrats have spent years attempting to tear away those commonalities in favor of coalitional interest-group politics. They've declared American philosophy racist from inception; they've declared American history a litany of brutalities; they've declared American culture bigotry embodied. Now they want unity—the unity of absolute victory.

Ironically, it's that very desire—the desire for monolithic control—that will be their undoing. Unless Biden is serious about unity—unless he's willing to cross the aisle and recognize the humanity of those with whom he disagrees, and to call out those on his own side who won't—Biden's term is likely to be contentious, polarizing and ultimately unsuccessful.

They Want to Shut You Up

November 18, 2020

This week, Abigail Shrier, author of the new book "Irreversible Damage: The Transgender Craze Seducing Our Daughters," found herself at the center of a firestorm. Her great crime: writing an assessment of the psychological phenomenon known as rapid onset gender dysphoria, where groups of psychologically vulnerable young girls begin to self-diagnose as transgender after one member of a peer group does so. The book is sober and evenhanded. Nonetheless, all hell broke loose after one person on Twitter—one!—tweeted at Target, prompting the retailer to pledge not to make Shrier's book available (a decision it later reversed).

This wasn't Shrier's first turn in the barrel. When the book first came out some months back, Amazon quickly moved to prevent her from advertising it, although books openly stumping for hormone treatment for minors suffering from gender dysphoria have met no such ban. This time, however, the publicity began to rage out of control. A transgender Berkeley professor called for burning the book, arguing, "all you're doing is removing a commodity from circulation—much as one might destroy a contaminated crop." Chase Strangio, deputy director for transgender justice at the American Civil Liberties Union, decided to abandon any pretense about defending civil liberties, tweeting, "stopping circulation of this book and these ideas is 100% a hill I will die on."

Meanwhile, the email service Mailchimp, which handles mass emails on behalf of organizations, announced it would no longer work with the Northern Virginia Tea Party, stating that it was promoting "potential ... misinformation" by holding a rally calling for a vote recount. Similarly, Facebook has reportedly been suppressing all information related to the possibility of voter fraud; so has Twitter.

Such niceties aren't reserved for the political right. Matthew Yglesias, co-founder of Vox, left his own publication this week for Substack after explaining that there was a "damaging trend in the media" toward treating "disagreement as a source of harm or personal safety." That trend, Yglesias stated, made it "very challenging to do good work."

Those who refuse to abide by prevailing leftist norms often find alternative outlets. But such avenues of escape are then attacked as well. This week, the Columbia Journalism Review ran a piece targeting Substack for the great sin of hosting material that might be deemed unworthy among leftist thinkers. It questioned whether Substack would "replicate the patterns of marginalization found across the media industry," condemning the company's founders for their view that many viewpoints ought to be given access to the system. And CNN found time to attack Parler, a conservative answer to Twitter, with Brian Stelter lamenting that "people are going more and more into their own echo chambers." Which is somewhat ironic, given the enormous echo chamber CNN represents.

The goal here isn't a freer discussion. It's precisely the reverse. Conservatives have known this for a long time, which is why they've had to operate using unconventional media such as talk radio and podcasting and startup websites. But the future of the country rests largely on a simple question: Will traditional liberals go along with the left, which seeks to silence, in order to achieve their favored policy prescriptions? Or will they walk away from the left and choose instead to engage in open conversation with conservatives, preserving freedom of thought and discussion but risking the possibility that their favorite policies will become more difficult to achieve?

That question remains unanswered for now. But time to answer it is running out. If we hope to have a country together moving forward, we'd better have an open conversation now.

Biden's 'Return to Normalcy' Is Going to Be Terrible

November 25, 2020

After spending two years avoiding serious questions about his policy preferences, his team and his prospective presidency, we now know what Joe Biden intends to do should the Electoral College, as expected, vote for him in December: He'll reopen the swamp for business. The media spent four long years suggesting that President Donald Trump was steeped in corruption, ensconced in partisanship, enmeshed in dangerous foreign policy fiascos. The media assured us that they would defend democracy from Trump's brutalities, that they would spend every waking moment fighting to prevent anyone from accepting Trumpian standards as the "new normal."

Instead, the media suggested we needed to return to the old "normal"—by which they meant a system in which the media and Democrats worked hand-in-glove together to lie to the American public about the content of policy ("If you like your doctor, you will be able to keep your doctor!"—former President Barack Obama); in which conventional wisdom was treated as gospel truth, no matter how wrong it was ("There will be no advanced and separate peace with the Arab world without the Palestinian process"—John Kerry on Israel); and in which cozy relationships between corporations and government were considered *de rigueur*.

They meant a system in which all difficult political questions were put off for another day; in which scandals were brushed off without a second thought; in which even anti-journalistic efforts by Democrats were dismissed as out of hand. It was a system in which constitutional boundaries were routinely overridden in the name of left-wing policy priorities; in which nasty rhetoric by Democrats was written off as a natural byproduct of the right's innate evil; in which alternative news sources were treated as conspiracy outlets.

That's the "normal" the media and Democrats wanted.

And it's the normal they'll apparently be pursuing. Biden is stacking his administration with all the members of the establishment Democratic gang. Tony Blinken, most famous for embracing the Iran deal and encouraging more American troops in Syria, will be headed to the State Department. Janet Yellen, fresh from her tenure as Federal Reserve chairwoman under Obama, will be headed to the Department of the Treasury. Jake Sullivan, Biden's national security adviser when he was vice president, most famous for the suggestion that the Iran deal was a stellar piece of negotiation (it wasn't), will become the White House national security adviser.

Meanwhile, the media will continue to cover Biden in sycophantic fashion. This week, The Washington Post ran an entire piece devoted to the wonders of the New Biden Era, titled "Washington's establishment hopes a Biden presidency will make schmoozing great again." The piece celebrated the old normal as "respect for experience and expertise," as "civility and bipartisan cooperation," as an opportunity to "bring people back together." One wonders what sort of peyote the editorial staff of The Washington Post must be ingesting in order to remember the Obama Era so fondly; then, one quickly realizes that they're simply high from huffing Democratic flatulence.

The old normal wasn't good. That's why Donald Trump was elected. It's why Democrats nearly lost the House, and why they seem poised to not take back the Senate despite Trump's personal unpopularity. The old normal stank of cronyism and oligarchy, of corrupt relationships between the Democratic infrastructure and the Democrats' praetorian guard in the media.

Today, the media celebrate the return of the old normal. That celebration is likely to again result in a backlash they can't control. And they'll be just as puzzled as ever about why everyone else wasn't as overjoyed as them about the return of the establishment Democratic swamp.

The Left's Gender Theories Are Anti-Scientific Nonsense, but They're Gaining Ground

December 2, 2020

On Nov. 22, 2020, New York Times columnist Charles Blow unleashed one of the most bizarre tweets in recent memory. "Stop doing gender reveals," he stated. "They're not cute; they're violent. All we know before a child is born is their anatomy. They will reveal their gender. It may match your expectations of that anatomy, and it may not. If you love the child you will be patience, attentive and open."

This is patently insane for a variety of reasons.

First, the characterization of gender reveal parties—parties during which parents celebrate finding out whether their unborn children are boys or girls—as "violent" is, in and of itself, radically nuts. Parents are excited to learn whether their children will be boys or girls. That is absolutely unobjectionable. But for an ardent fan of abortion on demand such as Blow to characterize a gender reveal party celebrating the sex of an unborn baby as "violent" while characterizing the *in utero* dismemberment of that same unborn baby as "choice" is so morally benighted as to boggle the mind.

Blow's tweet goes further. The implication that parents are doing violence against their own children if they connect sex and gender is utterly anti-evidentiary. Sex and gender are interconnected. For nearly every human being born, biological sex will correspond with genital development in the womb. And gender, contrary to the idiotic, pseudoscientific paganism of the gender theory set, is not some free-floating set of biases we bring to the table. Males and females have different qualities in a variety of functions, attitudes, desires and capabilities. In every human culture—indeed, in every mammalian species—meaningful distinctions between male and female remain. To reduce children to genderless unicorns simply awaiting hormonal guidance from within piles absurdity upon absurdity.

And, of course, Blow's take on "patience" is not limitless. Presumably, should your daughter announce that she is a boy at the tender age of 5, all measures will immediately be taken to ensure that she is treated as a boy by those such as Blow. There will be no call for watchful waiting; to do so would be yet another act of "violence."

Why does any of this matter? Because Blow's perspective has become mainstream on the left. In October, Healthline, a supposed medical resource, ran an article reviewed by a licensed marriage and family therapist titled "'Do Vulva Owners Like Sex?' Is the Wrong Question—Here's What You Should Ask Instead." Whether "vulva owners" like sex is indeed the wrong question. The right question, to begin, might be what makes "vulva owners" distinct from women; as a follow-up, we might ask how one would go about leasing or renting a vulva if ownership seems like too much of a burden.

But the madness gains ground. CNN reported in July that the American Cancer Society had changed its recommendations on the proper age for cervical cancer screenings for women, only CNN termed women "individuals with a cervix." Which seems rather degrading to women, come to think of it.

Lest we believe that this is merely some lunatic fringe, it is worth noting that Blow, Healthline and CNN are merely saying out loud what those who place gender pronouns in their Twitter bios, such as Vice President-elect Kamala Harris, imply: that gender and sex are completely severable, and that biology has nothing to do with the former. President-elect Joe Biden has openly stated that an 8-year-old can decide on his transgenderism; Sen. Elizabeth Warren infamously stated that she would have a 9-year-old transgender child screen her secretary of education nominee. Male and female are arbitrary categories to which anyone can claim membership.

Unless, of course, the left wishes to treat sex as an important characteristic. Then the logic changes. Thus, it is historic that Biden has nominated an all-female communications team, and it is deeply moving that Harris is a woman.

It's almost as though the definitions of words have no meaning, according to the left. All that matters is fealty to whatever narrative the chosen moral caste dictates on a daily basis. And if you cross it, you're doing violence.

Don't Let COVID-19 Lockdowns Become a Permanent Power Grab

December 9, 2020

This week, as Los Angeles County announced it would lock down all outdoor dining, a video went viral. That video featured restaurant owner Angela Marsden, proprietor of the Pineapple Hill Saloon and Grill, decrying the lockdown policy while pointing to the erection of production catering set up for a Hollywood shoot just a few feet away. "Everything I own is being taken away from me, and they set up a movie company right next to my outdoor patio," Marsden said, adding that she has spent approximately $80,000 complying with the requirements of LA County, only to see it shut down her business completely.

There is no scientific policy justifying LA County's outdoor-dining shutdown. In fact, during a Board of Supervisors meeting, a community member quizzed LA County Health Officer Dr. Muntu Davis on the evidence to support such a ban. Muntu provided no such evidence, likely because there is none.

But those who want to run their businesses in a safe and secure fashion are being targeted nonetheless by a political class incentivized to pursue tyranny rather than rational policy. LA Mayor Eric Garcetti—who told police to stand down as rioters tore through his city during a pandemic—said that his "heart goes out to Ms. Marsden" and then added, "No one likes these restrictions, but I do support them as our hospital ICU beds fill to capacity." He explained, "We must stop this virus before it kills thousands of more Angelenos." He did not explain why, if outdoor dining was so dangerous, Hollywood is still allowed to engage in it.

That's no surprise. Throughout the pandemic, one set of rules has applied to America's most ardent lockdown advocates, and another set of rules has applied to everyone else. LA County Supervisor Sheila Kuehl voted to ban outdoor dining ... and then went to an outdoor restaurant later that evening. California Gov. Gavin Newsom is currently locking down some 33 million citizens but had no problem eating *indoors* with members of the California Medical Association at The French Laundry. Mayor London Breed of San Francisco ate at that same posh restaurant the next day. Austin Mayor Steve Adler told his constituents, "stay home if you can" in a Facebook video filmed from his vacation timeshare in Cabo San Lucas, where he'd just headed with seven others after a wedding in Austin. Mayor Lori Lightfoot of Chicago got her hair cut and called it an "essential" business activity while promoting lockdown. Gov. Andrew Cuomo told everybody to stay home for Thanksgiving and then announced he would be getting together with his daughters and his 89-year-old mother, only to then reverse himself.

The message is obvious: Our intellectual and moral betters in politics are free to make their own rational calculations on COVID-19 risk. The rest of us are to be locked in our homes until further notice. When these political actors suggest that we must act out of an abundance of caution, they mean that they ought to enjoy abundance while benefitting from our caution.

You and your family are capable of making the same decisions Cuomo, Garcetti, Newsom, Lightfoot and Adler do. You *should* be careful; you should engage in social distancing, mask up when in close proximity with others and generally avoid social gatherings involving those with preexisting conditions. But you can do all of these things and still live in a free society. Our politicians don't believe that, because our politicians have seen how easily so many Americans were willing to indefinitely suspend their freedoms out of trust in our authorities. Until the incentive structures change, our freedoms will continue to be throttled by people who have no problem exercising their own.

One need not be a COVID-19 skeptic in order to question whether the enthusiastic authoritarian streak revealed by those politicians can be curbed. The longer we tolerate it, the more our politicians will normalize their power grabs.

Revenge of the Lapdogs

December 16, 2020

For four years, we heard that President Donald Trump is a threat to freedom of the press. The Washington Post signaled its own faux bravery by adopting the slogan "Democracy Dies in Darkness" at the top of its masthead. CNN began running commercials about facts being facts, and apples being apples rather than bananas (unless, presumably, those apples identify as bananas). The New York Times championed its own supposed stunning intrepidity in covering the Trump administration.

Those four years followed eight years during which the sitting president of the United States, Barack Obama, treated the press as lapdogs. He fed them occasional treats; they licked his hand. He occasionally disciplined them; they learned silence. He asked them to bark on cue; they did. During the Obama era, scandals went underreported; egregious seizures of power were portrayed as inevitable byproducts of Republican intransigence; and Obama's political opponents were treated as deplorable remnants of historic American bigotry.

With the elevation of Joe Biden as president-elect, prepare for some hard-hitting deja vu.

To be fair, the extent of the media's lapdogging for Biden became clear throughout the election cycle. President Donald Trump was presented as the single-greatest factor in the rise of COVID around the nation. Barrels of ink were spilled over his supposed support for white supremacy. Reams of paper were wasted claiming that Trump presented a threat to the integrity of the election itself.

Biden, meanwhile, answered few, if any, difficult questions during the entirety of his campaign. In fact, when the New York Post reported on the contents of a laptop purportedly owned by Hunter Biden—emails and texts that spell out the possibility that Joe Biden knew about Hunter's nefarious global business activities trading on the Biden name—the media immediately worked to shut down the story. NPR announced it wouldn't cover the story, with managing editor Terence Samuel stating, "We don't want to waste our time on stories that are not really stories, and we don't want to waste our listeners' and readers' time on stories that are just pure distraction." Social media quickly came to heel, with Twitter banning the Post's account for weeks and Facebook announcing it would suppress distribution of the story.

Just a few weeks after the election, news broke that Hunter Biden had been under some form of federal investigation since 2018. Now the media see fit to cover Hunter's business activities—but only from the angle that his activities may provide some sort of challenge for his father's administration.

Meanwhile, the establishment media rush to defend Jill Biden from the supposedly cruel predations of a Wall Street Journal op-ed columnist who noted—correctly—that she should stop using the title "doctor," since she has an Ed.D., a doctorate in education, from the University of Delaware. That rather uncontroversial notion was met with a paroxysm of rage from the usual media suspects, many of whom deemed it misogynist.

It's no wonder that after Joe Biden's Electoral College victory speech, the man himself sneered at Fox News reporter Peter Doocy for asking him about Hunter. "Thanks for the congratulations," said the supposedly avuncular Biden sarcastically. "Appreciate it."

It wasn't Doocy's job to congratulate Biden. It was his job to ask Biden tough questions. But Biden could be forgiven for thinking otherwise. After all, the media have spent years demonstrating that they represent the public relations wing of the Democratic Party, rather than acting as the staunch guardians of objective truth they purport to be.

The Perversion of Science

December 23, 2020

America's scientists are essentially miracle workers. Within mere months, they have developed highly effective vaccines for COVID-19. By year's end, millions of Americans will have received their first doses. We should begin to see death rates from COVID drop precipitously in the coming weeks as more and more Americans gain immunity from the virus.

Yet never has there been a larger gap between America's scientists and America's public health professionals. Science is supposed to guide the decision-making for both groups. Yet public health professionals have consistently failed to utilize science as their lodestar, instead sacrificing their credibility on the altar of intersectional politics. Throughout the summer, public health professionals ignored perfectly obvious dangers surrounding mass protests over alleged racial injustice; many of those top health professionals suggested that the risks of racism in American society amounted to a health problem all their own. Throughout the pandemic, public health officials have caved to the political incentive toward overbroad lockdown policies, simultaneously exempting themselves from the rules.

Now we learn that public health officials pushed for vaccine distribution not based on health risk but on racial factors. As the U.K.'s Daily Mail reported this week: "Every US state has been advised to consider ethnic minorities as a critical and vulnerable group in their vaccine distribution plans, according to Centers for Disease Control guidance. As a result, half of the nation's states have outlined plans that now prioritize black, Hispanic and indigenous residents over white people in some way."

This insanity is rooted in eugenic concerns. "Older populations are whiter," public health "expert" Dr. Harald Schmidt of the University of Pennsylvania told The New York Times in early December. "Society is structured in a way that enables them to live longer. Instead of giving additional health benefits to those who already had more of them, we can start to level the playing field a bit." In other words, a disproportionate number of white people survive to old age; we should, therefore, give vaccines to younger, less vulnerable nonwhite citizens in "essential industries" and let Grandma die.

Not only is this obviously racist; it happens to engender policy that kills more black people in absolute terms. Age is a far better predictor of COVID vulnerability than race: As Dr. Gbenga Ogedegbe of the New York University Grossman School of Medicine found, infected patients die at the same rate regardless of race. This means that if you give tranches of the vaccine to patients based on racial concerns rather than age concerns, the most vulnerable black and Latino populations—elderly blacks and Latinos—are more likely to die so that younger black and Latinos can receive a vaccine for a disease to which they are probably 10 times less vulnerable.

This is the price of social justice thinking. By treating people as members of racial groups rather than as individuals, and by prioritizing race above age, more black and brown people die in absolute terms, even if the overall proportionality of black and brown deaths drops versus white deaths. "Equitable" statistical outcome has become a higher goal than actually saving lives.

That's absurd and tragic. And it should undermine our trust in our public health officials. So, trust the scientists when they root their decisions in science. But doubt them at the top of your lungs when they start proclaiming that they are experts on morality.

About the Author

Ben Shapiro was born in 1984. He entered the University of California Los Angeles at the age of 16 and graduated summa cum laude and Phi Beta Kappa in June 2004 with a Bachelor of Arts degree in Political Science. He graduated Harvard Law School cum laude in June 2007.

Shapiro was hired by Creators Syndicate at age 17 to become the youngest nationally syndicated columnist in the United States. His columns are printed in major newspapers and websites including The Riverside Press-Enterprise and the Conservative Chronicle, Townhall.com, ABCNews.com, WorldNetDaily.com, Human Events, FrontPageMag.com, and FamilySecurityMatters.com. His columns have appeared in The Christian Science Monitor, Chicago Sun-Times, Orlando Sentinel, The Honolulu Advertiser, The Arizona Republic, Claremont Review of Books, and RealClearPolitics.com. He has been the subject of articles by The Wall Street Journal, The New York Times, The Associated Press, and The Christian Science Monitor. He has been quoted on "The Rush Limbaugh Show" and "The Dr. Laura Show," at CBSNews.com, and in the New York Press, The Washington Times, and The American Conservative.

Shapiro is the author of best-sellers "Brainwashed: How Universities Indoctrinate America's Youth," "Porn Generation: How Social Liberalism Is Corrupting Our Future," and "Project President: Bad Hair and Botox on the Road to the White House." He has appeared on hundreds of television and radio shows around the nation, including "The O'Reilly Factor," "Fox and Friends," "In the Money," "DaySide with Linda Vester," "Scarborough Country," "The Dennis Miller Show," "Fox News Live," "Glenn Beck Show," "Your World with Neil Cavuto," "700 Club," "The Laura Ingraham Show," "The

Michael Medved Show," "The G. Gordon Liddy Show," "The Rusty Humphries Show," "The Lars Larson Show," "The Larry Elder Show," The Hugh Hewitt Show," and "The Dennis Prager Show."

Shapiro is married and runs Benjamin Shapiro Legal Consulting in Los Angeles.

2020: Every Column Ben Shapiro Wrote During an Insane Year
is also available as an e-book
for Kindle, Amazon Fire, iPad, Nook and
Android e-readers. Visit
creatorspublishing.com to learn more.

∘ ∘ ∘

CREATORS PUBLISHING

We find compelling storytellers and
help them craft their narrative,
distributing their novels and collections
worldwide.

∘ ∘ ∘

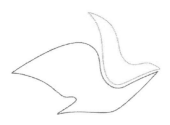

Made in the USA
Monee, IL
26 October 2021